The Attention Trader

Strategies for Success in Day Trading

SIMON MALCOM

Contents

Introduction 8
Chapter 1: Foundations of Day Trading 12
    Essential Tools and Technologies 14
    Why use day trading gear? 15
    6 Day Buying And Selling Equipment 16
    Effective Trading Environment 19
    Optimizing Your Trading Environment 20
Chapter 2: Developing a Trading Strategy 22
    Understanding Trading Strategies 23
    Creating a Personal Trading Plan 24
    Identifying Key Market Indicators 27
    Market Indicators – Types 29
    Risk Management and Capital Preservation 33
    What Are Some Common Types of Systematic Risk? .. 35
    Systematic Risk Management Techniques 36
    Capital Preservation Strategies 38
Chapter 3: Enhancing Focus and Discipline 39
    Understand the Power of Discipline 39
    Set Clear Goals and Stick to Your Plan 40
    Continuous Learning and Adaptation 42

Develop a Routine 42

Mindfulness Techniques for Traders 43

Chapter 4: Technical Analysis 52

Past Price as an Indicator of Future Performance 52

Charting on Different Time Frames 53

Candlesticks 56

Candlestick Patterns – Dojis 58

Technical Indicators – Moving Averages 61

Fibonacci Retracements 63

Fibonacci Extensions 65

Technical Indicators – Momentum Indicators 67

Using Technical Indicators Effectively 69

Moving Averages 70

How to use the MACD to gauge the trend? 74

Relative Strength Index (RSI) 75

How to apply the RSI to gauge the trend? 77

On-Balance Volume (OBV) 78

How to apply the OBV to gauge the fashion? 79

Advanced Technical Analysis Techniques 81

Bullish engulfing sample 81

Bearish engulfing sample 83

Bullish divergence signal 85

Bearish divergence sign 87

The false breakout 88

Chapter 5: Fundamental Analysis 90

Understanding Market News and Reports 91

Types of Market News and Reports 92

Significance of Market News and Reports 94

Analyzing Corporate Earnings Reports 97

Trade Agreements and Tariffs 98

Understanding Market Sentiment Reports 99

Utilizing Analyst Reports and Recommendations 100

Practical Tips for Using Market News and Reports 101

Economic Indicators and Their Impact 103

Integrating Fundamental Analysis into Your Strategy 110

What Is Fundamental Analysis in Trading? 111

How To Use Fundamental Analysis Effectively 113

Chapter 6: Trading Psychology 116

The fundamentals of dealer psychology 116

The significance of growing a buying and selling psychology
.... 119

Can bias affect a dealer's psychology? 122

How to enhance your trading psychology? 126

Learning from Losses and Wins 127

The Importance of Learning from Losses and Wins.............128

Strategies for Learning from Losses....................................129

Strategies for Learning from Wins 132

Balancing Learning from Both Wins and Losses 135

Chapter 7: Real-time Trading Strategies...................................137

Scalping Strategies for Quick Profits 138

Price movement scalping method 140

High-frequency scalping approach 142

Spotting Trends in Swing Trading 146

Tools for the Swing Trader..146

Swing Trading Risks and Rewards 147

Thrive inside the Fast Lane of Day Trading 148

Techniques for Day Trading Success 149

Day Trading Risks and Rewards 150

Speculating for Profit in Futures 152

Liquidity in the Futures Market 153

Futures Market Risks and Rewards..153

Charting Your Trading Journey 154

Chapter 8: Automation and Algorithms 156

How Algorithmic Trading Works 156

Advantages and Disadvantages of Algorithmic Trading 157

Building and Testing Automated Strategies 161

Test Automation Strategy 161

Objectives of Test Automation Strategy 162

Test Automation Strategy Example 164

Achieved 5x quicker QA automation 165

Benefits of Test Automation Strategy 168

Best Practices to Build a Test Automation Strategy 178

Pros and Cons of Automated Trading 184

Conclusion 189

Disclaimer

The facts furnished on this book is for instructional purposes simplest. The author and publisher aren't financial advisors and are not liable for any economic choices made based on the information furnished in this eBook. All buying and selling includes hazard, and readers must seek expert recommendation earlier than making any trading choices.

© 2024 **SIMON MALCOM** All rights reserved.

Introduction

Day-buying and selling interest involves strategically capturing, retaining, and leveraging the attention of a target audience on social media structures. Much like financial day buying and selling, where the aim is to make earnings by taking gain of marketplace fluctuations inside a single day, day-trading interest specializes in short-time period techniques to draw and interact customers constantly, preserving them hooked and converting their engagement into tangible consequences together with logo loyalty and income.

I inadvertently carried out an interesting experiment the day gone by at the same time as buying and selling. I traded from an enclosed office that become absolutely quiet and free of distraction. Interestingly, it truly is just like the placing wherein I generally behavior my meditation and biofeedback work. Indeed, after I work on preserving comfortable, awareness the usage of biofeedback gadget, I pick out an remoted placing that lets in me to maintain an unbroken focus. The ensuing "quarter" kingdom is one that I actually have determined to be helpful for clarity of concept and selection-making.

So in trading from the eliminated office, I unwittingly recreated my cognitive gym surroundings. Within a few minutes of following the market, I located myself doing *exactly* what I do in biofeedback: slowing my respiratory, making it greater rhythmical, keeping nonetheless, sustaining a excessive diploma of consciousness, and shutting off maximum inner speak.

What I determined became that, in this country, market motion regarded slower and clearer than traditional. When I am distracted--and especially if I'm frustrated--it appears as although I'm several steps at the back of the marketplace. Things appear earlier than I make sense of market behavior, so I'm in a reactive mode. When I turned into inside the region throughout the day past's trading, I felt on top of what the marketplace turned into doing, in which I was feeling the flow of shoppers and dealers. I changed into not considering shopping for, selling, earning profits, losing money, or P/L. I was utterly immersed within the ebb and drift of what the marketplace changed into doing. At instances, it felt as even though I become one with the market. In fact, the feeling become very similar to the feeling I've had whilst doing self-hypnosis sporting events.

Relatively early in the session, the marketplace pulled back and I may want to feel the attempts at promoting fail to push charges lower. I stated out loud to myself, "We cannot spoil the outlet lows. The customers are in control." That turned out to be a key perception for the day's trading.

Trading psychology professionals emphasize the need to govern emotion and bad thinking at some point of trading, and I assume that is vital. Emotional self-discipline is essential for desirable buying and selling, however perhaps now not enough. What I became moreover gazing became that a kingdom of hyper-focus and superior concentration absolutely changed me enjoy of the marketplace in addition to my processing of marketplace-associated facts. In essence, I had grown to become the trading consultation into a biofeedback consultation and the calm attention changed how I considered and spoke back to marketplace hobby. I did not plan trades; I certainly joined the waft of interest and exited when that flow shifted.

What if brief-time period trading is a feature of sample recognition and pattern popularity hinges upon our state of awareness? How a whole lot effectiveness can we lose in buying and selling with the aid of dividing our interest and so watering down our consciousness that we in no way honestly enter the "quarter" of facts processing? When we are first rate-targeted, perhaps we create a cognitive environment wherein trading psychology issues *cannot* dominate.

Chapter 1: Foundations of Day Trading

Day trading entails regularly shopping for and selling securities at some point of the trading day. Day traders attempt to count on and make cash from intraday price changes in belongings like shares, bonds, commodities, and exchange-traded finances.

As the name shows, day buying and selling is a brief-term funding strategy. The purpose is to exit all your trades with the aid of the stop of the day, conserving no securities in a single day.

Contrast this method to long-time period making an investment, wherein you buy and maintain the identical role for months—or even years. Instead of looking ahead to time and compound interest to do the work for them, day traders attempt to beat the marketplace and generate short income.

While day trading may additionally appear exciting and profitable, it's far effectively playing with all the capability upsides and risks you'd have having a bet via every other street. It calls for a high level of hazard tolerance and a incredible deal of exercise to get right. Commission-unfastened on-line dealer money owed have made day trading lots easier and value effective. In the past, you wished to name a stockbroker to make trades. Not only became this very time-eating, but it additionally fees you a lot more in keeping with alternate. In addition, beginner investors did now not have easy get right of entry to marketplace facts.

Today, the best on-line brokerage systems like Interactive Brokers or Trade Station let you execute trades quick from home, with a lot lower costs. Most fee no commissions on inventory and ETF trades, as well as many other varieties of securities. They also provide reams of detailed marketplace facts totally free.

Once you have your brokerage account installation, it'll come up with get entry to shop for and sell investments. It would also give you get entry to several research gear like charts, marketplace information, scanners and inventory screeners.

As an afternoon trader, you perceive the markets and investments you want to cognizance on. You then try to shop for and promote at some stage in the day to time positions that make you money, which include buying a stock proper earlier than a declaration pushes the fee up and then selling as soon as you observed the charge hits the height.

Top on-line brokerage structures will let you automate some of the procedure the usage of exclusive order sorts, consisting of limits on how tons of a stock you'll purchase at what price, and bounds on what you'll sell a inventory for. For instance, you may set up your account to shop for a hundred shares of XYZ inventory if it ever hits $20.00 a proportion and to sell your one hundred shares if it ever hits $25.00 a share.

Essential Tools and Technologies

Day trading tools are industry-unique packages or add-ons that assist day buying and selling experts in their responsibilities. They may assist secure the most present day stock marketplace data and provide records important for their choice-making. These gear commonly consist of various styles of software program, electronic devices, calculators and technology that help carry out calculations, music statistics and analyze facts.

These gear regularly allow day investors to boom their activity performance by means of supplying them with benefits and possibilities, together with distinctive insights into the inventory market, that they wouldn't have otherwise. They can be in particular useful to amateur day buyers who do not have as plenty enjoy with traits and forecasting.

Why use day trading gear?

You might also use day buying and selling gear for a wide form of reasons, together with:

Performing calculations

Facilitating inventory trades

Determining which stocks to change

Storing and saving certain monetary assets

Researching market and economic tendencies

Moving price range

6 Day Buying And Selling Equipment

There are a variety of one of a kind day trading gear that expert can use of their work. These tools range from electronic and virtual gear to manual gear and normally include:

1. Stock-scanning software

Day buyers often use useful inventory-scanning software to assist them in locating particular shares to exchange. This sort of software program generally permits day buyers to set standards and specifications that perceive which shares to exchange. They can look for standards such as largest gainers or losers, quantity spikes and bull flags.

2. Online brokers

Day traders want an internet broker to facilitate their trades and permit them to characteristic of their position. In maximum cases, professionals in this role have get right of entry to to several on-line brokering equipment, with the intention to use the one that exceptional suits their specific inventory alternate wishes. Financial groups normally provide on-line brokering tools and software program for day investors to select from, but they may set higher commissions and offer less customization. Smaller regulated brokers may offer lower fee or 0-fee buying and selling. Brokerages use exclusive sorts of software and have get right of entry to to extraordinary markets, so make inquiries before choosing.

3 Stock market dashboard

Being capable of view different factors of the stock market in any respect points in time is commonly a need for successful day buying and selling. Because of this, day traders regularly use stock market dashboard tools that collect day by day stock and marketplace records and present it in a single without problems viewable and handy dashboard. This allows for a easy and green method of growing focus of modifications within the stock marketplace.

4 Digital calculators

Both easy and superior clinical calculators are crucial for acting day trading calculations. Professionals in this function often have each varieties of digital calculators effortlessly handy to perform quick calculations and decide how a good deal money they may generate or lose when buying and selling shares. Typically, day traders have those gear both on their computers and their mobile gadgets, together with their drugs and smartphones, for instant get admission to.

5. Day buying and selling software

Day buying and selling software is one of the crucial every day tools of an afternoon dealer. This software helps the trading of stocks and motion of price range. There are usually numerous varieties of software that day buyers use to help them reach their role, which include:

Charting software program

Online brokering software program

Scanning software program

6. News dashboards

It's regularly essential for day traders to display any breaking news because it relates to the stock marketplace. Doing so can boom their cognizance of market and economic fluctuations and the reviews of area professionals. Because of this, day investors frequently use information dashboard gear that compile distinctive information web sites so experts can without problems.

Effective Trading Environment

Creating some surroundings optimized for buying and selling fulfillment is greater than simply tidying up your desk. A clutter-free space promotes readability and tranquility but, you may take steps past that to stay centered for your buying and selling goals. Minimizing distractions, whether it's from noisy neighbors, a passing train, or consistent notifications, permits you to pay attention completely to your trading consultation and optimize productivity.

Investing for your buying and selling environment demonstrates your dedication to achievement. It suggests that you price developing the right conditions for achieving your desires, boosting your self-belief and motivation. By retaining a targeted mind-set thru a tranquil workspace, you may enhance your performance and usual nicely-being within the trading global.

Optimizing Your Trading Environment

Here are a few recommendations to help your installation a comfortable and green trading space:
Comfortable Chair: Invest in an amazing chair that supports your posture and allows you hold attention.
Adjustable Desk: Consider a desk that lets in for sitting and status to hold you snug and engaged.

Proper Lighting: Ensure exact lights to reduce eye stress. Don't overlook that the warm temperature of the light matters!

Multiple Monitors: Consider the use of more than one screens to decorate productivity.
Cable Management: Keep your workspace tidy and secure by means of organizing cables to avoid distractions.

Noise Control: Create a quiet surroundings. Either pick out a quiet area or use noise-cancelling headphones or soundproofing materials.

Clutter-Free Workspace: Use organizational equipment to keep your workspace organized for a clean mind.
Some matters are greater achievable and low-priced steps to take than others. Choose the stairs that fit your needs and your price range first-rate, and have the most impact in your workspace.

Chapter 2: Developing a Trading Strategy

A trading strategy is a systematic method used for purchasing and selling within the securities markets. A buying and selling strategy is based totally on predefined policies and standards used when making buying and selling selections.

A buying and selling approach may be easy or complex, and involve issues such as funding fashion (e.g., value vs. Increase), market cap, technical indicators, fundamental evaluation, industry sector, degree of portfolio diversification, time horizon or protecting length, danger tolerance, leverage, tax considerations, and so on. The secret is that a buying and selling method be set using objective records and analysis and is adhered to diligently. At the equal time, a trading method ought to be periodically re-evaluated and tweaked as marketplace situations or person desires change.

Understanding Trading Strategies

A trading approach includes a properly-considered investing and buying and selling plan that specifies making an investment goals, risk tolerance, time horizon, and tax implications. Ideas and exceptional practices need to be researched and followed then adhered to. Planning for buying and selling consists of growing techniques that consist of buying or promoting stocks, bonds, ETFs, or other investments and can extend to greater complex trades which includes options or futures.

Placing trades approach running with a dealer or broker-dealer and figuring out and managing buying and selling costs inclusive of spreads, commissions, and fees. Once done, trading positions are monitored and managed, along with adjusting or ultimate them as wanted. Risk and go back are measured in addition to portfolio impacts of trades and tax implications.

Creating a Personal Trading Plan

No trading plans are the identical due to the fact no investors are precisely alike. Each technique will reflect vital factors like trading fashion in addition to risk tolerance. What are the different vital additives of a solid buying and selling plan? Here are 10 that every plan ought to encompass:

1. Goal Definition

Firstly, if you are new to buying and selling, you should determine financial goals, danger tolerance, and time horizon. These objects want to be without a doubt articulated to ensure that your trading sports may be completed.

2. Trading Style Selection

A trading fashion needs to be recognized. This style ought to replicate your character, tradition and alternatives. The plan can encompass day buying and selling, swing buying and selling, function trading or lengthy-term investing. The selected fashion ought to align with one's dreams and time availability.

3. Strategy Development

A special strategy needs to be created. This approach outlines an approach to the markets. Also a criterion for exchange selection wishes to be defined. This can include technical indicators, essential evaluation or a aggregate of both. Finally, while constructing the approach, entry and exit processes, risk management techniques, and function sizing policies need to be distinctive.

4. Realistic Expectation Setting

Trading is not a assured route to wealth and includes inherent dangers. Realistic expectancies for returns need to be set and the ability for losses needs to be diagnosed. You should keep away from the lure of chasing quick profits or risking too much capital on a unmarried role or trade.

five. Comprehensive Market Analysis

You want to behavior thorough market evaluation to discover ability trade possibilities. If they're part of your plan, analyze charts, market tendencies need to be studied, information and monetary signs ought to be monitored. Take a step again and don't forget the overall market circumstance.

6. Risk Management Rule Development

In order to protect capital, danger control techniques need to be carried out. Allocate a percent of your portfolio for every alternate and don't go above the quantity you've got determined is right to your account. This amount need to be equal to the quantity that you are inclined to lose in line with exchange. Make use of forestall loss-orders to limit potential losses and set up clear take income goals to stable profits.

7. Trade Management Plan

Determine how you will manipulate open positions. You ought to decide when to alter prevent-loss orders, take partial profits (in all likelihood thru the use of trailing stops), or exit the exchange absolutely.

8. Trading Discipline Maintenance

Once you have got written your trading plan down, stay with it, avoid situations in which you abandon your buying and selling plan impulsively because the market is doing something that elicits an emotional reaction from you like fear or greed. Train yourself to embody field and consistency whilst executing and exiting trades.

9. Monitoring and Trade Evaluation

A particular file of buying and selling interest, inclusive of entry and exit points, motives for taking the exchange, and the consequences are essential. A frequent review and evaluation of trades is necessary to becoming an amazing dealer. The assessment and evaluate of your beyond trades will permit you to perceive patterns, strengths, and regions for improvement.

Identifying Key Market Indicators

Market indicators are much like technical signs in that each practice a statistical method to a series of information factors to attract a end. The difference is that marketplace signs use information factors from a couple of securities as opposed to only a single safety. Often instances, market indicators are plotted on a separate chart as opposed to performing above or below an index price chart.

Most inventory market signs are created with the aid of studying the variety of corporations which have reached new highs relative to the wide variety that created new lows, referred to as market breadth, since it indicates wherein the overall trend is headed.

The most commonplace styles of marketplace indicators are:

Market Breadth indicators compare the variety of stocks transferring in the identical route as a bigger fashion. For instance, the Advance-Decline Line looks on the variety of advancing stocks as opposed to the variety of declining shares.

Market Sentiment signs compare charge and extent to determine whether or not traders are bullish or bearish on the overall market. For example, the Put Call Ratio looks at the wide variety of positioned alternatives versus name alternatives at some stage in a given period.

Here's an instance of the NASDAQ Advance-Decline Issues index:

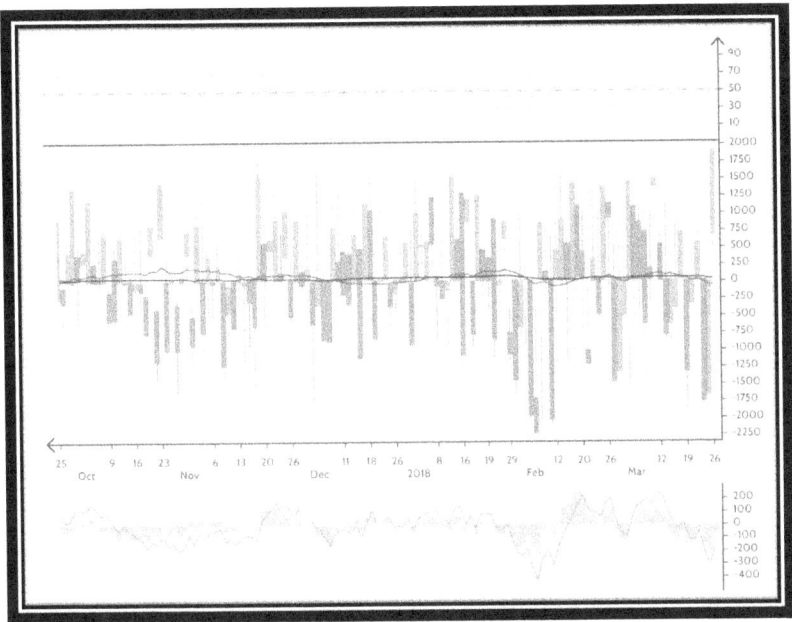

Market Indicators – Types

There are multiple kinds of market indicators. Common indicators include the following:

1. Market Breadth

Market breadth signs compare information of numerous stocks that show a comparable charge movement. It enables investors to examine where the fashion is headed within the near destiny. The number of groups that attain new highs may be as compared with the wide variety of stocks that attain new lows inside a given trading length.

The market breadth is beneficial for fashion investors who broadly speaking searching for to earnings off betting on developments of charge moves in the market. Trends are taken into consideration to be noticeably no-danger if the signs used are correct, and chance is well accounted for. However, developments do now not account for trading psychology, that may purpose surprising price movements inside the marketplace.

For example, the enhance-decline line is a ratio that considers the range of definitely advancing shares in an index in place of the stocks that are negatively advancing.

The indicator is beneficial because it consists of the weight of the marketplace capitalization of a given company while calculating the trajectory of charge moves, in place of clearly thinking about the fee moves of the stock of the biggest agency in that index. Common examples include $NYAD and $NAAD.

2. Market Sentiment

Market sentiment indicators serve to assessment the fee of a safety with its quantity of change. It is executed so one can determine if, on the overall market, traders are bullish or bearish on the overall marketplace.

For instance, the positioned-call ratio calculates the wide variety of call alternatives rather than the number of placed alternatives bought in a given period.

3. Moving Averages

Moving averages are useful in filtering out irrelevant information factors in that they "easy" out available rate records. It is due to the fact a transferring common is expressed as a single flowing line that represents the average rate of a given security over a period.

The selected length is up to the discretion of the trader, depending upon their priorities. For instance, buyers and long-time period trend followers will usually remember a time-frame of 50, one hundred, or 200 days. Short-term buyers may recall a week-long period.

The shifting average can indicate numerous homes in the trajectory of a given security. The angle of the slope can reveal the trend line. A horizontal shifting average suggests that the rate of the security varies at the same time as a definitely sloped shifting common indicates that the rate is probable to upward thrust.

It is critical to notice that shifting averages do no longer are expecting price movements, but in reality show the actual price moves that have already passed off. Examples include $NYA50, $NYA200, $NAA50, and $NAA200.

four. On-Balance Volume (OBV)
Volume of change is an important market indicator, and on-stability extent collates quite a few quantity-associated records into a single flowing line. OBV doesn't predict price movements however confirms developments. A growing OBV indicates that the fee of the safety is growing whilst a bad OBV accompanies negative price actions.

If the OBV and fee are moving in contrary instructions, the rate motion is possibly to change its route. A growing OBV observed by means of a falling price suggests that the fee may quickly start to rise. A falling charge observed by using an OBV this is flat lining way that the price is nearing a backside.

Risk Management and Capital Preservation

One of the motives nearly all monetary recommendation takes diversification with no consideration is that it's miles the maximum sincere defense against person asset volatility – the low hanging fruit of basic threat control, if you may.

But the danger of massive losses isn't fully mitigated by using diversification on my own. Diversification is only a start line. To mitigate towards large losses (like those experienced through many investors in 2022, as an example), wealth managers and investors need to pick investment strategies and price range that contain capital protection measures.

Below, we ruin down how traders can recognize systematic risks and offer some examples of investment strategies that could mitigate exposure to massive losses of their funding portfolio.

Understanding and Managing Systematic Risk

Systematic risks are risks related to crisis across a big number of sectors of the economic system or of the monetary device itself. They are the opposite of idiosyncratic risks, which might be specific to individual agencies, industries or asset lessons. Systematic dangers encompass economy-huge crises that have negative results for all investors.

Probably the most excellent current examples of systematic chance are the Great Recession (GR) in 2008–2009 and the COVID pandemic crash of 2020. In the GR, the bursting of a bubble in a single unique sector that led to a worldwide monetary downturn might also appear strange. But turbulence within the housing market — starting with the subprime mortgage market — created dangers and economic consequences a way outside one enterprise.

What Are Some Common Types of Systematic Risk?

Systematic dangers range in their reasons but are comparable in their effect; they produce considerable exposure to losses due to the fact they have an effect on entire economies or the financial device itself.

Common systematic dangers include:

Market Risk – Any huge-scale changes to the marketplace will impact almost all investors. Market threat is interchangeable with systematic chance.

Currency Risk – Normal oscillations in currency exchange rates are to be anticipated, however irregular fluctuations could have huge, economy-huge, influences on import and export prices and consequently sincerely all goods and offerings.

Interest Risk – Interest prices reason two inversely associated varieties of systematic danger. The first, reinvestment danger, is whilst reinvesting dividends could earn much less within the future. And the second one, fee dangers, stand up whilst higher interest fees drive asset expenses down.

Inflation Risk – Also referred to as shopping strength hazard, this refers both to clients' capacity to guide the economy and the real effect of portfolios' funding earnings.

Political and Regulatory Risk – Governmental moves together with declarations of struggle, new regulatory measures, or bailouts can reason major ripple outcomes across all asset types.

Managing systematic dangers manner coping with a portfolio in a way that minimizes publicity to the large potential losses those risks can impose.

Systematic Risk Management Techniques

The most direct way to deal with systematic risks in a fund or investment method is to account for and comprise them deliberately. Applying the additives above approach a few mixtures of:

Asset Allocation – As previously noted, diversifying away systematic risks appearance specific from diversifying away idiosyncratic risks. It calls for taking a whole lot of systematic dangers into attention throughout asset instructions and locating methods to reap uncorrelated security overall performance while these risks take place.

Active Risk Management and/or Hedging – A greater strict application of dynamic chance allocation continually balances higher-beta investments with decrease-beta ones, aiming to keep the preferred/goal beta (danger exposure) for each risk factor.

Risk Monitoring and Review – Fund managers also can follow similarly analytical rigor to their portfolios, past CAPM-fashion betas, which may additionally tend to result in a rather static view of what is in reality an ever-evolving hazard surroundings for a portfolio. For example, real-time proprietary studies into belongings and their diverse danger exposures may additionally produce a portfolio with progressed capital preservation traits.

Capital Preservation Strategies

Funds and techniques with capital maintenance traits prioritize disadvantage loss mitigation and normally this implies having a nicely-oiled, sophisticated, quantitative method to threat management which could balance capturing opportunities with navigating towards massive losses over marketplace cycles.

Some techniques on this vein consist of:

Dynamic Risk Allocation – Adjusting portfolio exposures as had to preserve a fund inside it goal danger envelope always.

Defensive Investment Approaches – Focusing on portfolio production wherein the forms of belongings (or portfolio composition) are selected for their capability to decrease loss and maximize stability amidst market-extensive crises. Low volatility price range would be an instance of protecting making an investment.

Chapter 3: Enhancing Focus and Discipline

Day buying and selling may be an exciting and probably worthwhile undertaking, but it calls for discipline and the development of sturdy behavior.

In this Chapter, we are able to discover the significance of buying and selling with discipline and percentage sensible suggestions to help you build the behavior important for day trading success.

Understand the Power of Discipline

Discipline is the inspiration of successful day trading. It involves sticking to a fixed of predetermined guidelines and techniques, regardless of feelings or outside impacts. With subject, you may keep away from impulsive decisions and keep a consistent method to buying and selling.

Set Clear Goals and Stick to Your Plan

Define your trading goals and set up a properly-idea-out buying and selling plan. Your plan must include access and go out techniques, risk control techniques, and hints for position sizing. By adhering for your plan, you can keep away from hasty decisions pushed through fear or greed.

Practice Patience

Patience is a virtue in day buying and selling. It is important to look forward to excessive-chance buying and selling opportunities that align along with your strategy. Avoid chasing trades or forcing trades whilst the market conditions are not favorable. Patience allows you to make well-calculated decisions and increases the likelihood of worthwhile trades.

Embrace Risk Management

Effective danger management is vital for long-time period fulfillment in day buying and selling. Set a maximum risk in step with change, usually a percent of your trading capital, and stick with it. This enables guard you from full-size losses that could negatively affect your universal buying and selling overall performance. Additionally, consider utilizing prevent-loss orders to restriction capability losses and trailing stops to protect income.

Maintain Emotional Control

Emotions can be damaging to day buying and selling fulfillment. Fear and greed can cloud judgment and result in impulsive choices. It is critical to apprehend and manipulate those emotions. One effective technique is to establish predefined guidelines for entering and exiting trades, getting rid of the need for subjective selection-making primarily based on feelings.

Analyze and Learn from Your Trades

Regularly evaluation and examine your trades to gain insights into your strengths and weaknesses. Keep a buying and selling journal to record the information of each exchange, which include the cause behind your choices, entry and go out factors, and the outcome. Analyzing past trades helps identify patterns and regions for improvement, allowing you to refine your strategies over the years.

Continuous Learning and Adaptation

The market is dynamic, and staying updated is critical. Engage in continuous getting to know by means of analyzing trading books, attending webinars, and following authentic financial information assets. Additionally, be open to adapting your trading strategies as market conditions alternate. Flexibility and a willingness to examine will help you live in advance inside the ever-evolving trading landscape.

Develop a Routine

Establishing a daily routine can sell field and consistency to your buying and selling. Create a dependent time table that consists of market studies, chart analysis, change execution, and post-alternate evaluation. By following a recurring, you can expand a centered mindset and keep the important field to reach day trading.

Trading with field is fundamental to accomplishing lengthy-term achievement in day buying and selling. By constructing sturdy conduct, such as putting clean desires, working towards persistence, embracing hazard management, and preserving emotional control, you may navigate the markets with confidence and consistency.

Remember, field is a ability that can be cultivated through the years, so be patient and chronic to your journey closer to becoming a disciplined day trader.

Mindfulness Techniques for Traders

In the short-paced and competitive international of buying and selling, where each second counts, the idea of mindfulness is out of place. Nevertheless, this time-honored area, that's based on the idea of being absolutely gift and engaged in the cutting-edge moment, is being widely stated as a strong instrument for buying and selling. Your potential to make decisions and your typical performance can be stepped forward via gaining a expertise of mindfulness and making use of it for your trading exercise. This is genuine regardless of whether you are just starting or have years of understanding.

Understanding Mindfulness

Mindfulness can be likened to possessing a unique device that aids in carefully observing the existing moment with none desire for it to be altered. It's all about taking note of the small information - the feeling of your breath because it enters and exits your body, the manner your frame feels even as sitting or status, or even the diverse sounds that surround you. It's all about being absolutely centered and mindful, comparable to immersing yourself in a movie and gazing every complex factor on the display screen without being sidetracked with the aid of thoughts of plans.

By enticing within the practice of mindfulness, you are honing your cognitive abilities to concentrate entirely at the modern moment. It's just like using a magnifying glass to look at something up close; you examine a plethora of intricate info that would in any other case move left out with a casual look. Mindfulness operates further, albeit with a focus on introspection rather than external commentary. It includes diligently attending to one's mind, feelings, and bodily reports.

Through the practice of mindfulness, individuals can increase the capability to technique various situations with a more experience of tranquility and a reduced tendency to react hastily. Instead of turning into instantly dissatisfied or pressured by something, you permit yourself a brief pause to determine your desired reaction. It's much like hitting the "pause" button, supplying you with the possibility to pick your reaction.

Practicing mindfulness can shift your perspective, allowing you to fully embody the prevailing second, effectively manipulate your feelings, and cultivate self-compassion. It's similar to owning a hidden sanctuary within your thoughts, a tranquil safe haven that stays undisturbed with the aid of outside occasions.

Breathing practice

Here's an easy breathing approach you could deliver a shot:
Find a cozy spot in a nonviolent environment, lightly shut your eyes, and permit yourself to hook up with your physical presence fully.

Inhale deeply thru your nostrils, taking a peaceful and measured breath. Let your stomach enlarge as you achieve this.

Take a second to pause, and then gently let loose a sluggish breath through your mouth, allowing any stress or distractions to melt away.

Continue working towards this deep respiration method for a few minutes, directing your attention entirely to the revel in of your breath flowing inside and outside of your frame.

Engaging in this respiration technique previous to and in the course of your buying and selling classes assist you to locate inner stability and preserve a lucid and concentrated country of mind.

Meditation for Scanning the Body

Another powerful mindfulness method for traders is the body scan meditation. This technique entails methodically directing your recognition to various areas of your body, commencing from your ft and ascending to the crown of your head. Here's a way you can test with:

Find a cozy spot to relax, whether or not it is lying down or sitting in a chair along with your ft planted firmly on the ground. Take a second to shut your eyes gently.

Begin with the aid of directing your interest toward your ft. Observe any emotions, traces, or regions of calmness in that specific location without attempting to modify something.

Slowly shift your recognition upwards, starting out of your ft. and progressing in your ankles, calves, knees, and beyond. Take word of everybody component and allow go of any strain or strain you stumble upon.

Keep repeating this method until you reach the best point of your head, softly analyzing your frame and focusing on every place.

Participating in a thorough frame scan meditation previous to your trading sessions can assist in relieving physical tension and fostering a experience of grounding, that can in the end beautify your clarity and awareness.

Practices for Mindful Trading

Incorporating mindfulness into your trading sports can significantly enhance your ordinary trading enjoy. Here are a few guidelines to combine mindfulness into your buying and selling strategies:

Observe market actions without forming reviews: Pay near interest to the marketplace without assigning any emotional value to the fluctuations. Adopt a curious and independent angle.

Trade with cautious attention: Prior to executing a alternate, pause and mirror for your intentions to confirm they may be in line with your buying and selling strategy. Take a second to connect to yourself and renowned your feelings.

Remember to take ordinary breaks: In the midst of the quick-paced buying and selling surroundings, ensure to schedule quick pauses to step far away from the display screen, take deep breaths, and refocus your mind.

By incorporating mindfulness into your buying and selling habitual, you can cultivate a heightened kingdom of attention and intellectual readability. This will assist you steer clear of impulsive or emotionally charged decisions, ensuring a more rational and calculated approach.

Overcoming Emotional Biases

The mental elements of market timing largely decide whether or not a dealer is a success or unsuccessful. Emotions including worry, greed, and overconfidence can reason illogical selection-making and hinder the capacity to enforce timing strategies effectively.

Let's appearance particularly at how to overcome emotional ideals thru mindfulness:

Cultivate a deep understanding of oneself

Be aware of and well known your emotional biases and the way they can affect your trading selections. Consistently observe your mind, emotions, and movements at some point of buying and selling, and understand ordinary patterns of emotional impact that could be impacting your timing techniques.

Adhere to a Trading Strategy

Create a properly-described and thorough trading plan that simply outlines your strategies for timing the market, standards for entering and exiting trades, rules for coping with danger, and plans for handling sudden conditions. Please stick to your plan constantly and withstand the temptation to stray from it due to emotional urges or out of doors pressures.

Developing persistence and discipline is important

Develop a experience of staying power and strength of will for your buying and selling method, and steer clear of making hasty picks inspired through your feelings. Be affected person and watch for the suitable opportunities that suit your buying and selling method. Avoid making impulsive decisions primarily based on marketplace changes or the have an effect on of others.

Embrace the unknown

Embrace the fact that unpredictability is a herbal thing of market timing and that experiencing losses is an unavoidable element of buying and selling. Embrace a mind-set that acknowledges the function of probability and prioritizes risk control over the pursuit of absolute truth whilst making timing choices. Embrace the unknown as a threat to benefit know-how and expand your competencies to your trading journey.

Incorporate Mindfulness Practices

Utilize various mindfulness strategies, like targeted breathing, contemplation, or intellectual imagery, to correctly cope with stress and uphold emotional equilibrium during trading. Remain absolutely engaged inside the gift second, carefully observe your thoughts and feelings with none bias, and nurture a serene and concentrated mind-set that promotes making properly-timed decisions.

Chapter 4: Technical Analysis

Technical evaluation is a device, or technique, used to are expecting the probably future price movement of a security – including a stock or foreign money pair – primarily based on market statistics.

The concept behind the validity of technical analysis is the belief that the collective actions – buying and promoting – of all of the contributors in the marketplace as it should be reflecting all applicable data referring to a traded protection, and consequently, continually assign an honest market price to the safety.

Past Price as an Indicator of Future Performance

Technical traders trust that modern or beyond price movement inside the marketplace is the most reliable indicator of future rate action.

Technical analysis isn't always most effective utilized by technical traders. Many essential buyers use essential evaluation to decide whether or not to shop for into a marketplace, however having made that choice, then use technical evaluation to pinpoint suitable, low-hazard purchase access charge degrees.

Charting on Different Time Frames

Technical investors analyze fee charts to attempt to expect price motion. The two number one variables for technical analysis are the time frames taken into consideration and the particular technical signs that a dealer chooses to make use of.

The technical evaluation time frames proven on charts range from one-minute to monthly, or maybe every year, time spans. Popular time frames that technical analysts most often have a look at include:

five-minute chart
15-minute chart
Hourly chart
four-hour chart
Daily chart

The time frame a trader selects to look at is typically determined by means of that person trader's non-public trading fashion. Intra-day investors, investors who open and close trading positions within a single trading day, choose studying price motion on shorter time frame charts, such as the 5-minute or 15-minute charts. Long-time period traders who preserve market positions in a single day and for lengthy intervals of time are extra willing to research markets using hourly, four-hour, every day, or even weekly charts.

Price movement that occurs within a fifteen-minute time span can be very considerable for an intra-day dealer who's seeking out an opportunity to recognize a benefit from charge fluctuations occurring at some stage in one trading day. However, that same rate motion regarded on a day by day or weekly chart may not be particularly giant or indicative for lengthy-time period buying and selling purposes.

It's easy to demonstrate this by way of viewing the same charge motion on distinctive time body charts. The following daily chart for silver shows price trading inside the same range, from roughly $16 to $18.50, that it's been in for the beyond several months. A long-term silver investor might be willing to look to shop for silver primarily based on the truth that the price in all fairness near the low of that variety.

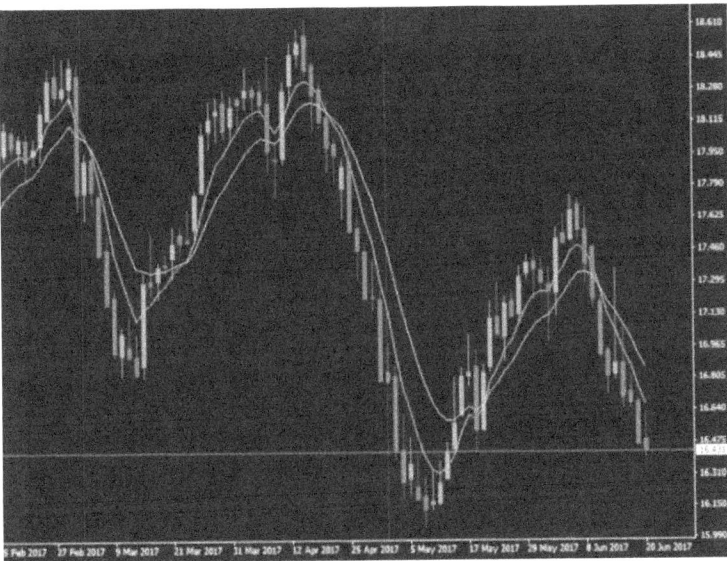

However, the same charge action viewed on an hourly chart (beneath) suggests a constant downtrend that has multiplied particularly simply in the past several hours. A silver investor interested best in making an intra-day alternate could likely shrink back from buying the treasured metallic primarily based on the hourly chart rate movement.

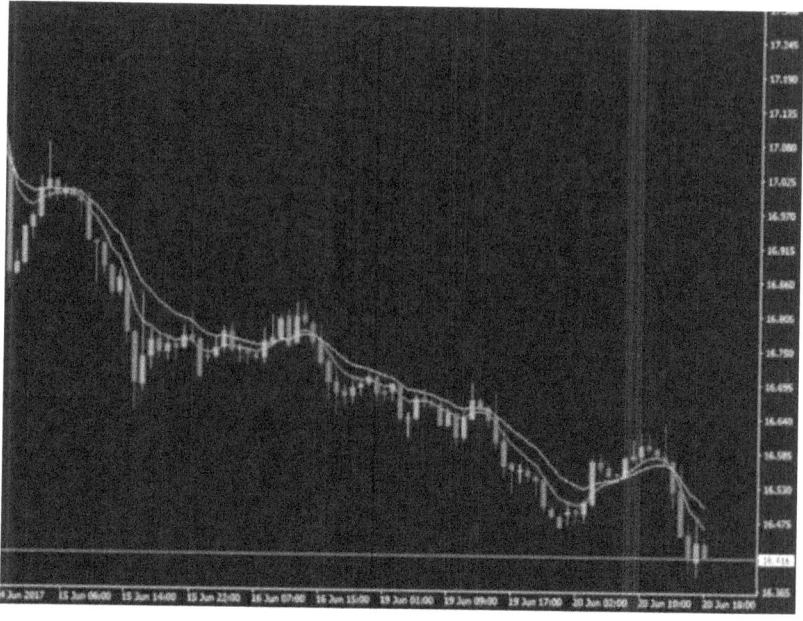

Candlesticks

Candlestick charting is the most usually used technique of displaying rate motion on a chart. A candlestick is formed from the rate movement at some point of a single term for any time body. Each candlestick on an hourly chart indicates the rate motion for one hour, at the same time as each candlestick on a 4-hour chart suggests the price movement at some point of every four-hour term.

Candlesticks are "drawn" / formed as follows: The highest point of a candlestick shows the best charge a safety traded at all through that term, and the lowest factor of the candlestick shows the lowest charge for the duration of that time. The "frame" of a candlestick (the respective crimson or blue "blocks", or thicker components, of every candlestick as shown in the charts above) indicates the opening and last fees for the term. If a blue candlestick frame is fashioned, this shows that the ultimate rate (top of the candlestick frame) changed into higher than the outlet charge (backside of the candlestick body); conversely, if a crimson candlestick frame is fashioned, then the outlet fee turned into higher than the last fee.

Candlestick shades are arbitrary selections. Some investors use white and black candlestick bodies (this is the default coloration format, and consequently the only maximum typically used); other buyers can also pick out to use green and crimson, or blue and yellow. Whatever colorations are chosen, they provide an clean way to determine at a glance whether rate closed better or lower at the give up of a given time period. Technical analysis using a candlestick charts is regularly less difficult than the use of a fashionable bar chart, as the analyst gets more visual cues and styles.

Candlestick Patterns – Dojis

Candlestick patterns, which can be fashioned with the aid of both a unmarried candlestick or by means of a succession of or three candlesticks, are a number of the maximum widely used technical signs for figuring out potential marketplace reversals or fashion exchange.

Doji candlesticks, as an instance, suggest indecision in a marketplace that is a sign for an forthcoming trend alternate or market reversal. The singular function of a doji candlestick is that the opening and remaining expenses are the identical, so that the candlestick frame is a flat line. The longer the higher and/or decrease "shadows", or "tails", on a doji candlestick – a part of the candlestick that indicates the low-to-high range for the time period – the more potent the indication of market indecision and potential reversal.

There are numerous versions of doji candlesticks, each with its own unique name, as proven inside the example beneath.

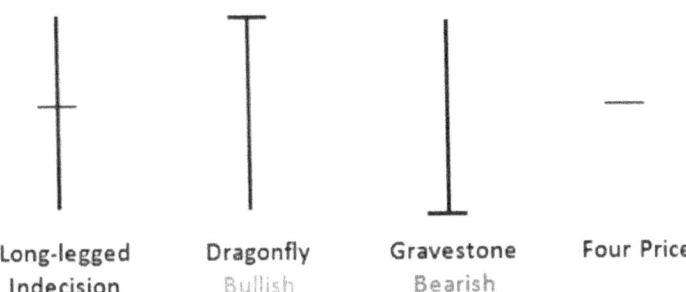

The common doji is the long-legged doji, wherein fee extends approximately equally in every course, establishing and final within the middle of the rate variety for the term. The look of the candlestick offers a clear visual indication of indecision inside the market. When a doji like this seems after an prolonged uptrend or downtrend in a marketplace, it's miles typically interpreted as signaling a probable market reversal, a trend change to the alternative course.

The dragonfly doji, while performing after a extended downtrend, signals a probable upcoming reversal to the upside. Examination of the charge action indicated by way of the dragonfly doji explains its logical interpretation. The dragonfly indicates dealers pushing rate significantly decrease (the long decrease tail), but on the cease of the length, charge recovers to shut at its highest point. The candlestick basically indicates a rejection of the extended push to the downside.

The gravestone doji's name really hints that it represents awful news for consumers. The contrary of the dragonfly formation, the gravestone doji suggests a robust rejection of a try and push marketplace prices higher, and thereby suggests a potential disadvantage reversal may additionally follow.

The rare, 4 rate doji, where the marketplace opens, closes, and in-among conducts all shopping for and selling at the precise same fee for the duration of the term, is the epitome of indecision, a marketplace that suggests no inclination to head everywhere specifically.

There are dozens of various candlestick formations, at the side of several sample versions. Probably the maximum entire aid for figuring out and utilizing candlestick styles is Thomas Bukowski's sample web page, which thoroughly explains each candlestick pattern and even affords statistics on how often each sample has historically given a dependable trading sign. It's clearly beneficial to realize what a candlestick pattern indicates – but it's even extra beneficial to understand if that indication has proven to be accurate eighty% of the time.

Technical Indicators – Moving Averages

In addition to reading candlestick formations, technical traders can draw from a definitely endless deliver of technical signs to assist them in making trading selections.

Moving averages are likely the single most extensively used technical indicator. Many buying and selling strategies make use of one or greater moving averages. A simple transferring common buying and selling strategy might be something like, "Buy so long as rate stays above the 50-duration exponential moving average (EMA); Sell as long as rate remains underneath the 50 EMA".

Moving average crossovers are every other frequently hired technical indicator. A crossover buying and selling approach is probably to buy whilst the 10-duration shifting average crosses above the 50-period shifting common.

The higher a transferring common range is, the greater considerable charge motion on the subject of its miles taken into consideration. For instance, charge crossing above or beneath a hundred- or 2 hundred-duration moving average is normally considered tons greater giant than rate shifting above or below a five-duration transferring common.

Technical Indicators – Pivots and Fibonacci Numbers

Daily pivot point signs, which usually additionally discover several assist and resistance degrees similarly to the pivot factor, are used by many traders to identify fee levels for entering or last out trades. Pivot factor degrees frequently mark substantial support or resistance ranges or the degrees in which buying and selling is contained within a range. If buying and selling soars (or plummets) thru each day pivot and all the related aid or resistance levels, that is interpreted by means of many traders as "breakout" trading so that it will shift marketplace prices drastically better or lower, within the course of the breakout.

Daily pivot points and their corresponding guide and resistance tiers are calculated using the previous buying and selling day's high, low, beginning and closing charges. I'd display you the calculation, but there's truly no need, as pivot point ranges are broadly posted each trading day and there are pivot point indicators you can simply load on a chart that do the calculations for you and display pivot ranges. Most pivot factor indicators show the day by day pivot point in conjunction with three help levels under the pivot factor and 3 fee resistance tiers above it.

Fibonacci Retracements

Fibonacci stages are any other famous technical evaluation tool. Fibonacci turned into a 12th-century mathematician who evolved a series of ratios this is very famous with technical investors. Fibonacci ratios, or ranges, are generally used to pinpoint trading opportunities and both exchange access and profit goals that get up at some stage in sustained trends.

The number one Fibonacci ratios are zero.24, zero.38, zero.62, and 0. Seventy-six. These are often expressed as chances – 23%, 38%, etc. Note that Fibonacci ratios supplement other Fibonacci ratios: 24% is the opposite, or the rest, of 76%, and 38% is the opposite, or the rest, of 62%.

As with pivot point levels, there are various freely available technical signs with the intention to routinely calculate and cargo Fibonacci degrees onto a chart.

Fibonacci retracements are the most often used Fibonacci indicator. After a safety has been in a sustained uptrend or downtrend for some time, there's often a corrective retracement inside the contrary direction earlier than fee resumes the overall lengthy-time period fashion. Fibonacci retracements are used to identify appropriate, low-hazard exchange access points in the course of one of these retracement.

For example, assume that the price of stock "A" has climbed progressively from $10 to $40. Then the inventory price begins to fall back a piece. Many investors will search for an excellent access level to buy shares for the duration of the sort of charge retracement.

Fibonacci numbers advise that in all likelihood price retracements will amplify a distance equal to 24%, 38%, sixty-two%, or seventy-six% of the uptrend move from $10 to $40. Investors watch these ranges for indicators that the marketplace is locating guide from where fee will begin growing again. For example, in case you had been hoping for a chance to shop for the inventory after approximately a 38% retracement in price, you might input an order to shop for across the $31 price degree. (The circulate from $10 to $forty = $30; 38% of $30 is $nine; $40 – $nine = $31)

Fibonacci Extensions

Continuing with the above example – So now you've offered the inventory at $31 and you're seeking to decide a profit goal to promote at. For that, you can look to Fibonacci extensions, which indicate how much higher price may additionally amplify whilst the general uptrend resumes. The Fibonacci extension degrees are pegged at expenses that represent 126%, 138%, 162%, and 176% of the unique uptrend circulate, calculated from the low of the retracement. So, if a 38% retracement of the original flow from $10 to $forty seems to be the retracement low, then from that price ($31), you locate the first Fibonacci extension level and ability "take income" target by way of including 126% of the original $30 pass upward. The calculation goes as follows:

Fibonacci extension level of 126% = $31 + ($30 x 1.26) =$ sixty-eight – giving you a target fee of $68.

Once more, you in no way clearly should do any of those calculations. You just plug a Fibonacci indicator into your charting software and it displays all of the various Fibonacci degrees.

Pivot and Fibonacci tiers are worth tracking even if you don't in my view use them as signs in your very own trading strategy. Because such a lot of buyers do base shopping for and promoting moves on pivot and Fibonacci degrees, if not anything else there's likely to be sizeable trading activity round the ones charge points, activity which could assist you better determine possibly destiny rate moves.

Technical Indicators – Momentum Indicators

Moving averages and maximum other technical signs are mainly focused on figuring out probably marketplace path, up or down.

There is another class of technical signs, but, whose principal purpose is not so much to decide market direction as to decide market energy. These indicators encompass such famous equipment as the Stochastic Oscillator, the Relative Strength Index (RSI), the Moving Average Convergence-Divergence (MACD) indicator, and the Average Directional Movement Index (ADX).

By measuring the strength of fee motion, momentum signs help buyers decide whether or not current fee movement much more likely represents rather insignificant, variety-bound trading or an actual, vast fashion. Because momentum indicators measure fashion strength, they are able to serve as early caution signals that a fashion is coming to an quit. For instance, if a safety has been buying and selling in a sturdy, sustained uptrend for several months, but then one or extra momentum signs alerts the fashion progressively losing energy, it may be time to consider taking earnings.

The 4-hour chart of USD/SGD under illustrates the cost of a momentum indicator. The MACD indicator seems in a separate window underneath the primary chart window. The sharp upturn inside the MACD starting around June 14th indicates that the corresponding upsurge in charge is a robust, trending move as opposed to only a brief correction. When rate begins to retrace downward fairly at the 16th, the MACD shows weaker charge action, indicating that the downward motion in charge does no longer have much electricity at the back of it. Soon after that, a robust uptrend resumes. In this example, the MACD could have helped offer reassurance to a consumer of the market that (A) the flip to the upside become a tremendous fee circulate and (B) that the uptrend changed into in all likelihood to resume after the fee dipped barely at the 16th.

Because momentum indicators typically best sign robust or vulnerable price motion, but now not trend direction, they may be frequently combined with other technical analysis signs as a part of an average trading approach.

Using Technical Indicators Effectively

Technical indicators are precious tools in both crypto and inventory investors' arsenals. These signs use modern-day and ancient information to resource traders in identifying styles, comparing market tendencies, and making greater informed trading selections. They additionally assist in comprehending the market and see buying and selling alerts. Furthermore, technical indicators can help buyers in creating information-pushed buying and selling plans and techniques whilst mitigating the impact of fear, uncertainty, and market hype.

Moving Averages

A shifting average (MA) is a technical analysis indicator used to clean out a cryptocurrency's quick-time period rate fluctuation by means of calculating an average over a particular term. It is a device buyers and analysts use to differentiate an asset's real fashion direction from regular market noise. In addition, swing traders use MA to apprehend capability market entry and go out factors and help and resistance degrees.

Moving averages are regularly categorized into easy moving averages (SMAs) and exponential moving averages (EMAs). The SMA sums an asset's final price over a certain duration and divides it through the wide variety of durations.

For instance, a ten-day SMA could sum up the expenses of the closing 10 days and then divide by using 10 to get the common. A new data set in SMA will displace the oldest information, which sets it apart from a primary average. For instance, if the SMA is calculated on a 5-day basis, the facts set will continually be up to date most effective to include the most recent five days.

On the alternative hand, an EMA emphasizes the latest information factors by assigning them better weightage and fee. It is greater responsive to fast rate fluctuations and reversals than SMA, which treats all facts inputs as equals.

Short-term traders want EMAs over SMAs due to their quicker rate projection. Moving averages are taken into consideration lagging indicators because they depend upon beyond charge facts. This makes them useful to investors when confirming a marketplace trend instead of predicting the marketplace motion.

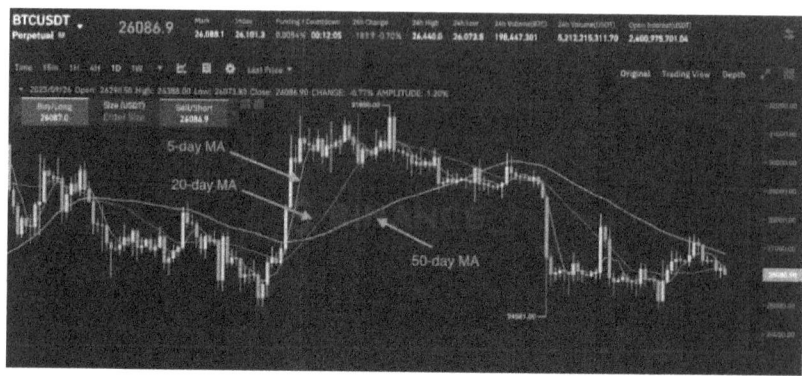

How to use Moving Averages to gauge the fashion?

There are three parameters to remember while including MA to charts:

Time Period: Periods like five-day, 10-day, 20-day, or 50-day for near-time period traits and a hundred-day, 200-day, or 500-day for long-term developments.

Price Type: The price to be able to be used to calculate the common, i.e., ultimate fee, low price, high rate, common of excessive and low costs, and many others.

MA Type: The type which includes easy moving averages and exponential moving averages formulas.

Example

Suppose an asset's 50-day Moving Average is $1,000, and it is presently buying and selling at $1,200. The upswing above the historic fee ($1,000) shows an upward trend. The new fee being above the MA indicates a superb investor sentiment and a probable expanded hobby within the asset.

Moving Average Convergence Divergence (MACD)

Moving common convergence divergence (MACD) is a momentum or oscillator indicator that compares wonderful moving averages of a crypto asset to apprehend a fashion's energy and its potential to reverse. Thus, it aids buyers in figuring out the route and momentum of a trend.

MACD is determined by finding the distinction between the 26-day EMA and the 12-day EMA. A 9-day EMA of the MACD is then plotted as a sign line. It is essential to note that the two traces on the chart show the distance or distance between the 2 EMAs (12-day and 26-day). It doesn't represent the EMAs themselves; as a substitute, it illustrates how a way apart they may be.

The sign line indicates the changes in price momentum and is considered a trigger for bearish and bullish alerts. A histogram often represents the distinction among the MACD and sign strains.

A decline in momentum and potential rate decrease is evident when the two MAs circulate closer to every different or converge. A divergence, or when the MAs flow faraway from each other, often shows an upward momentum and shows a bullish signal.

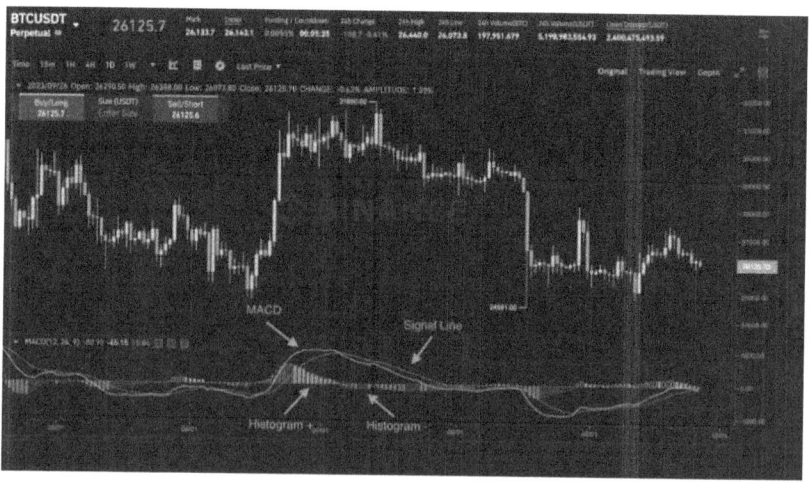

How to use the MACD to gauge the trend?
The parameters for MACD include the following:

Time Period: Typically makes use of 12-day and 26-day periods for its EMAs and a nine-day duration for its sign line.

Moving Averages: Relies on both brief-time period (12-day) and long-term (26-day) Exponential Moving Averages (EMAs).

Momentum: The gap among the two EMAs allows gauge the price momentum.

Example

Suppose you're monitoring an asset the usage of MACD.

If the MACD line crosses above the signal line, it indicates an upward momentum and a capacity buy possibility.

The MACD and signal line getting toward each different guidelines at a fashion reversal, i.e., short-time period trends are rapidly slowing down in comparison to long-time period traits. This signals a potential sell possibility.

Relative Strength Index (RSI)

The relative energy index (RSI) is one of the maximum normally used crypto buying and selling signs. It is used as a metric for the importance and electricity of a cryptocurrency's charge adjustments. RSI compares the size of an asset's most recent profits in opposition to its maximum recent losses. This enables buyers decide whether or not a cryptocurrency is oversold or overbought.

The RSI oscillator tiers between zero to one hundred, with a line graph shifting among the two extremes. A crypto asset with a studying above 70 indicators that the market is overbought and could suggest a charge correction. On the opposite, while the RSI oscillator reads below 30, it alerts an oversold marketplace and indicates a capability quit to the bearish fashion. A ability uptrend also can be diagnosed whilst the indicator breaks above the centerline and vice versa.

However, the RSI momentum indicator may additionally deliver false alerts, especially in trending markets. It is more appropriate for range-bound markets.

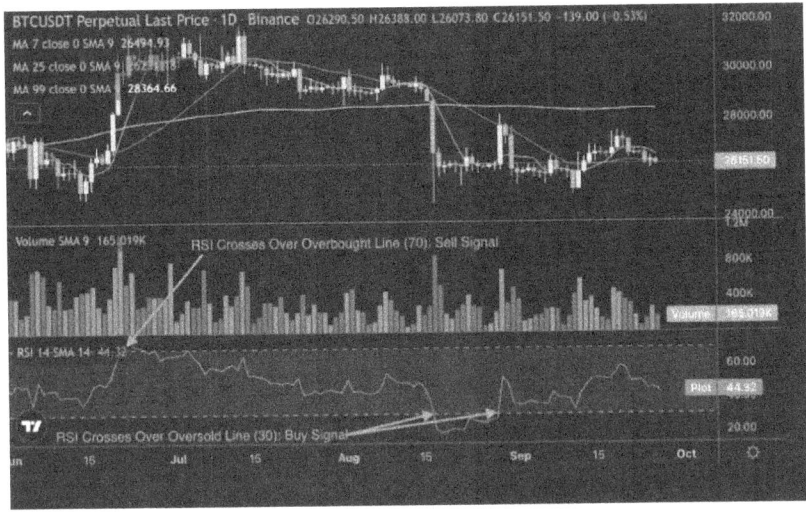

How to apply the RSI to gauge the trend?

The RSI parameters are:

Time Period: Usually used on a 14-day time-frame.
Oscillation Range: Ranges among zero to a hundred to indicate overbought (above 70) or oversold (underneath 30) situations.

Example

Suppose an investor is monitoring the RSI of an asset; if the RSI cost is:

Above 70: The asset is overbought (hyped up) or has experienced a surge in shopping for strain that drove the rate up. It should suggest a capability charge correction.

Below 30: The asset is oversold (undervalued) or has experienced a surge in selling stress and tips at a ability rebound.

On-Balance Volume (OBV)

On-balance extent (OBV) is a technical analysis indicator that tracks price and volume within the crypto market. It's a momentum device used to degree the float of quantity inside and outside of an asset, thereby suggesting the power or weak spot of fee moves.

The OBV works underneath the idea that when volume will increase sharply without a big change in the inventory's price, the charge will probably move upward, and vice versa. In essence, the on-stability volume indicator serves as a tool that uses quantity drift to predict adjustments in rate.

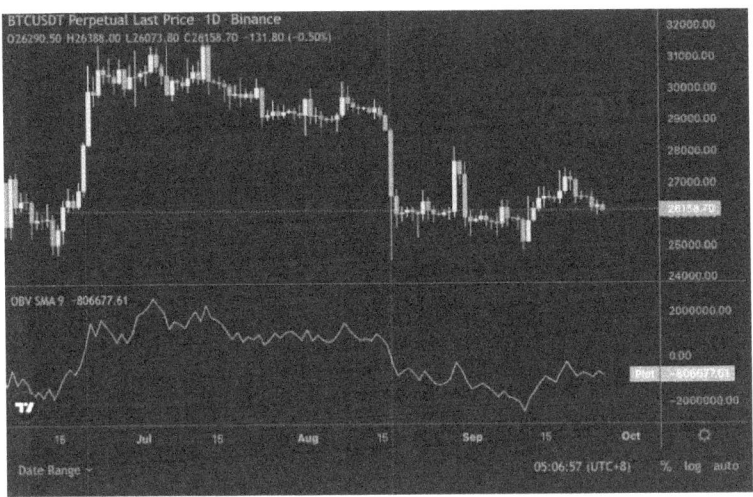

How to apply the OBV to gauge the fashion?

Volume: Volume plays a pivotal function inside the OBV because it measures the strength behind a charge pass. A massive exchange in charge accompanied through an excessive volume offers more weight to the charge pass, suggesting it is probably extra sustainable.

Price Direction: Depending at the asset's fee movement from sooner or later to the subsequent, extent is both added or subtracted:

If the present day price closes better than the day prior to this's near, the day's extent is introduced to the OBV.

If the cutting-edge price closes decrease than the day prior to this's near, the day's quantity is subtracted from the OBV.

Example

If the OBV starts to rise consecutively over some durations, it shows that volumes on up days are outweighing volumes on down days. This can recommend an upward price momentum and potentially a buy opportunity, especially if the asset's price is also growing. Conversely, if the OBV starts off evolved to say no over consecutive periods, it method volumes on down days are more than the ones on up days, indicating a downward rate momentum and potentially a sell signal, especially if the asset's rate is also declining.

If the asset's fee is growing, however the OBV is not following suit or is shifting in the opposite route, this divergence may also hint at a weakening of the continuing fashion, signaling a potential fashion reversal inside the near future. This can be a signal of warning for buyers.

Advanced Technical Analysis Techniques

Many investors use technical signs and charting analysis as an technique to examine the markets and notice capability trading possibilities and suitable entry and exit points. This article looks at 5 superior procedures to technical evaluation to help you improve your trading strategy.

Lots of investors use candlestick charts when looking at charge facts and it is straightforward to peer why. Candlesticks gift the warfare between consumers and sellers in a completely easy-to-interpret graphical manner. Candlestick charts also have their own variety of styles, with many focusing on the psychology of the market and constant struggle among consumers and dealers.

Bullish engulfing sample

The bullish engulfing sample happens when a market has been in a downtrend. Bullish engulfing styles normally encompass two whole candlesticks spanning time periods (for instance one hour or in the future). The first is a 'down' or bearish candlestick, followed by way of an 'up' or bullish candlestick protecting the following term.

The size of the primary candle can vary from chart to chart. The first candle typically signifies the cease of declining expenses for the markets. The 2d candle inside the sample must be larger than the preceding candle and ought to cover (or engulf) the 'frame' of the preceding candle. The bigger the second one candle and the higher it advances, the stronger the signal.

Here is an example of the FTSE 100 index based on day by day candlesticks.

In this situation, the marketplace has been falling for more than every week but there is a incredibly massive 'up' day that completely overshadows the day past's candle. These two candles together shape the bullish engulfing sample and advocate that weak spot is coming to a stop and the trend can be approximately to opposite.

Bearish engulfing sample

Bearish engulfing styles are a mirror photograph of the bullish variety, with the difference being that with bearish engulfing styles the market is heading higher, however then there's a candle within the opposite direction to the fashion which engulfs the preceding candle – signifying a alternate in sentiment from buying stress to selling stress.

As with the preceding candlestick chart pattern, the primary candle on this formation means that the contemporary fashion is coming to an cease. The size of the first candle can vary from chart to chart and it's far the second one or 'engulfing' candle that alerts the trade in trend. To qualify as a bearish engulfing pattern, the second one candle have to absolutely engulf the preceding candle. Ideally, the excessive have to expand above the previous candle's excessive and a brand new low have to be created – signifying renewed downward selling strain.

The underneath instance indicates the price of oil, and every candle represents one hour of buying and selling.

As with all different buying and selling techniques, candlestick charts need to be used together with other varieties of evaluation to weigh up whilst market sentiment may be shifting.

Bullish divergence signal

Many buyers will use technical indicators to discern out market course. You may additionally have seen charts with stochastic oscillators, transferring common convergence divergence (MACD) and different strains underneath the fee. One version of the indicator technique is to search for divergences. This is where the price does one factor but the indicator does something else – it is able to be a signal that a trend is jogging out of steam, supplying the opportunity to profit from a circulate within the different course. In the chart underneath, the price of gold has a relative strength index (RSI) shown below the rate, that is continually a famous indicator.

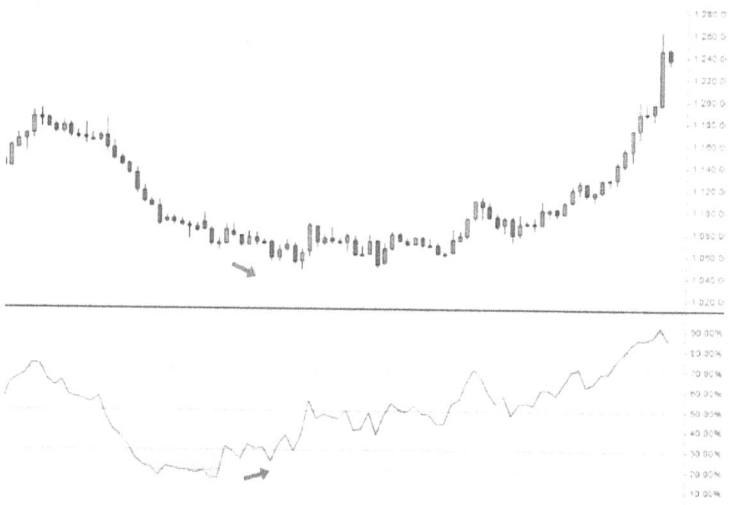

In the chart above, it can be visible that there's a good sized slide inside the charge of gold, as indicated via the pink and blue arrows, and the RSI becomes very oversold, pointing to how susceptible the marketplace has been. Later inside the identical month and the subsequent month, the rate of gold slips further, below those preceding lows. But curiously, the RSI has started out moving better. This is bullish divergence – and may be an offer that the downtrend is jogging out of steam, which proved to be the case in this case.

Bearish divergence sign

For every nice pattern there is mostly a bad opportunity and this is also the case in terms of divergence. When a market is making higher highs, however the RSI isn't always following suit, this is called 'bearish divergence' and may be a warning that a pinnacle is near. The instance underneath is an hourly chart for the GBP/USD foreign exchange pair. As indicated by the blue and purple arrows beneath, the market changed into sturdy toward the middle of the month but the RSI then makes a lower excessive than previously, suggesting that momentum may be starting to fade away.

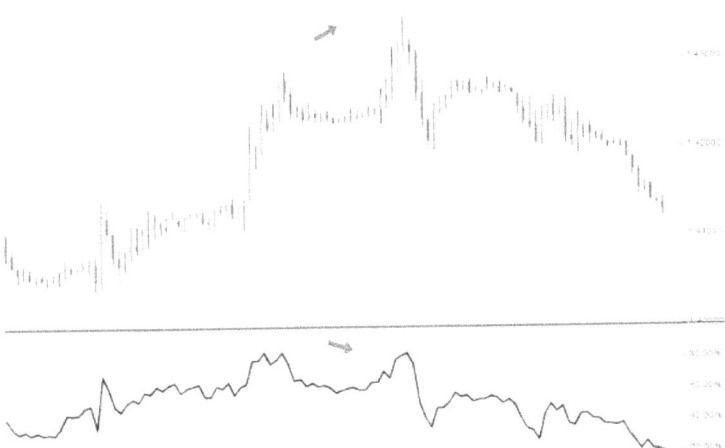

This divergence approach the use of indicators is notion to be more reliable than simply using them as simple overbought or oversold alerts. As ever, not anything works all the time but they could assist to 'take the temperature' of a marketplace and act as a caution that a previously good trend may be about to stall.

The false breakout

As cited before, no trading approach is right all of the time however even false alerts can deliver a touch into marketplace direction. The breakout approach is a popular one with momentum buyers: whilst a preceding low or excessive is broken at the chart a few will see it as the sign of a new fashion. But a whole lot of the time this doesn't manifest. This false breakout can still supply us an competitive trading method and is a beneficial bit of technical evaluation on its very own.

The US 30 index chart demonstrates this. The 17,900 level had acted as help over more than one days. The market then broke beneath this, but right away tried to regain its misplaced floor. There changed into no actual comply with-thru of selling. An aggressive trading method would be to shop for into this energy with a stop-loss order under the low following the wreck of that aid. False signals like this may come to be being effective. In this case weak sellers were flushed out and the marketplace ended up transferring one hundred fifty factors higher.

Chapter 5: Fundamental Analysis

Fundamental evaluation is a way of assessing the intrinsic fee of a stock. It combines economic statements, external affects, occasions, and industry trends. It is critical to be aware that the intrinsic fee or a honest fee of a inventory does not trade in a single day. Such evaluation helps you pick out key attributes of the company and examine its real worth, contemplating macro and microeconomic elements.

Fundamental analysis uses three sets of data:

historical facts to test how things had been in the beyond

publicly regarded information approximately the organization, consisting of announcements made by using the control and what others say approximately the organization facts that isn't acknowledged publicly however is beneficial, i.e., how the leadership handles crises, situations, and so on.

For an inventory, essential evaluation commonly consists of reviewing many factors associated with stock expenses, along with:

Performance of the general enterprise the corporation participates in

Domestic political surroundings

Relevant change agreements and outside politics

The agency's financial statements

The company's press releases

News releases associated with the employer and its business

Competitor evaluation

Understanding Market News and Reports

Market information and reports play a important function in shaping the selections of buyers and traders. By supplying insights into economic signs, corporate earnings, geopolitical activities, and marketplace sentiment, they assist marketplace participants make knowledgeable choices. In this complete guide, we're going to delve into the various styles of market information and reports, their significance, and a way to interpret them successfully.

Types of Market News and Reports

Economic Indicators

Economic indicators are statistical metrics used to gauge the overall health of an economy. They can be categorized into 3 principal classes: leading, lagging, and coincident indicators.

Leading Indicators

These predict destiny monetary hobby. Examples encompass the stock marketplace, manufacturing interest, and new commercial enterprise startups.

Lagging Indicators: These verify trends once they have started. Examples include unemployment charges, corporate earnings, and labor prices.

Coincident Indicators

These offer statistics approximately the cutting-edge kingdom of the financial system. Examples include GDP, industrial production, and retail sales.

Corporate Earnings Reports

Corporate earnings reviews are quarterly monetary statements issued with the aid of publicly traded corporations. They encompass key economic metrics together with sales, net earnings, income in line with percentage (EPS), and steering for future performance. These reviews are essential as they offer insights into a corporation's profitability, growth prospects, and monetary health.

Geopolitical Events

Geopolitical activities embody political, monetary, and social trends that may have an impact on market conditions. Examples encompass elections, exchange agreements, conflicts, and regulatory modifications. These activities can motive full-size volatility within the markets, making it crucial for traders to live informed.

Market Sentiment Reports

Market sentiment reports assess the general mindset of traders toward a particular market or asset. These reports may be based on surveys, social media analysis, or buying and selling interest. Market sentiment is frequently categorized as bullish (high quality) or bearish (poor).

Analyst Reports and Recommendations

Analyst reviews are produced by using monetary analysts who compare agencies, industries, or markets. These reviews include special evaluation, forecasts, and recommendations which include buy, maintain, or promote ratings. They are broadly observed and might have an effect on investor behavior.

Significance of Market News and Reports

Decision-Making

Market information and reviews offer the information necessary for making knowledgeable buying and selling selections. By studying this information, buyers can identify ability opportunities and risks, supporting them to increase techniques that align with their investment goals.

Risk Management

Understanding market news and reviews permits buyers to count on and control risks more efficaciously. For instance, knowing the release date of a main economic record or a enterprise's profits announcement can assist traders prepare for capacity market moves.

Market Sentiment

Market sentiment, regularly pushed by using news and reviews, can appreciably effect asset prices. Positive information can lead to extended shopping for interest, driving fees up, while bad news can trigger selling, causing fees to fall. By gauging marketplace sentiment, traders can higher be expecting and reply to marketplace actions.

Long-Term Trends

Market news and reports assist in figuring out lengthy-term financial and market developments. By knowledge those traits, investors could make strategic decisions that align with broader marketplace moves, instead of reacting to short-time period fluctuations.

Interpreting Economic Indicators

Gross Domestic Product (GDP)

GDP measures the whole cost of goods and offerings produced inside a country. It is a key indicator of economic fitness. A developing GDP shows a wholesome economy, whilst a declining GDP may additionally sign monetary issues. Traders observe GDP increase charges to evaluate the overall monetary trend and make funding decisions therefore.

Unemployment Rate

The unemployment rate is the percentage of the hard work pressure that is unemployed however actively in search of employment. A excessive unemployment charge suggests monetary misery, at the same time as a low rate indicates a robust process market. Changes within the unemployment rate can have an effect on client spending and financial boom, affecting marketplace conditions.

Inflation

Inflation measures the price at which the general degree of costs for goods and offerings is rising. Moderate inflation is normal in a growing economic system, but high inflation can erode shopping electricity and result in higher hobby costs. Central banks, just like the Federal Reserve, use inflation facts to set economic coverage, that may impact market interest rates and funding returns.

Consumer Confidence Index (CCI)

The CCI gauges purchaser sentiment regarding the financial system. High patron self-assurance shows accelerated spending and economic increase, while low confidence can indicate economic pessimism. Changes in consumer self-assurance can affect retail income and typical financial interest.

Analyzing Corporate Earnings Reports

Revenue and Net Income

Revenue represents the entire income generated via a business enterprise from its operations, at the same time as internet earnings is the income in any case expenses have been deducted. Rising revenue and net earnings imply a corporation's boom and profitability, making its stock more appealing to traders.

Earnings Per Share (EPS)

EPS is calculated by way of dividing a company's internet earnings with the aid of its number of fantastic shares. It offers a degree of profitability on a consistent with-percentage foundation. Higher EPS values are generally effective, indicating higher performance.

Guidance

Guidance refers to a agency's projections for future income and sales. Positive guidance can increase investor confidence and pressure up inventory charges, at the same time as bad guidance can result in sell-offs.

Impact of Geopolitical Events

Elections and Political Changes

Elections and political modifications will have sizable marketplace implications. For example, the election of a commercial enterprise-friendly authorities can raise investor self-belief, while political instability can cause market volatility.

Trade Agreements and Tariffs

Trade agreements can open new markets for businesses and enhance financial boom, even as price lists can restriction alternate and increase charges for corporations. Traders carefully screen traits in global exchange rules to assume their effect on markets.

Conflicts and Crises

Geopolitical conflicts and crises, together with wars or herbal screw ups, can motive uncertainty and marketplace volatility. Safe-haven assets like gold and authority's bonds frequently see elevated demand during such times.

Understanding Market Sentiment Reports

Sentiment Surveys

Sentiment surveys, along with the American Association of Individual Investors (AAII) Sentiment Survey, measure the temper of investors. A high percentage of bullish responses suggests optimism, while a excessive percent of bearish responses suggests pessimism.

Social Media and News Analysis

Analyzing social media developments and news headlines can provide insights into market sentiment. Tools like sentiment evaluation software program can song the frequency and tone of mentions related to precise stocks or markets.

Trading Volume and Volatility

High trading quantity and volatility can imply strong market sentiment. For example, a surge in trading volume at some point of a market rally suggests robust bullish sentiment, even as extended volume throughout a downturn shows bearish sentiment.

Utilizing Analyst Reports and Recommendations

Buy, Hold, and Sell Ratings

Analyst ratings offer hints on whether to shop for, preserve, or sell a stock. These rankings are primarily based on particular evaluation and can influence investor conduct. However, it is vital for investors to recall multiple analyst opinions and conduct their personal studies.

Price Targets

Analysts regularly set price objectives for shares, indicating their anticipated future price. These objectives are based totally on financial models and assumptions. While useful, investors must be conscious that fee goals are estimates and can be issue to trade.

Sector and Industry Analysis

Analyst reports additionally offer insights into unique sectors and industries. Understanding the wider industry trends can assist traders make extra informed decisions about person shares inside that sector.

Practical Tips for Using Market News and Reports

Stay Updated

Regularly observe legit monetary news sources, along with Bloomberg, Reuters, and The Wall Street Journal, to stay informed about marketplace trends. Subscribing to newsletters and signals also can assist you live on pinnacle of critical information.

Use Economic Calendars

Economic calendars list the release dates of key monetary reports and indicators. By tracking these dates, investors can put together for ability market actions and modify their strategies as a result

Diversify Information Sources

Relying on a unmarried source of information can cause biased choices. Diversify your facts resources to get a well-rounded view of the marketplace. This includes analyzing analyst reviews, following market sentiment indicators, and staying up to date on geopolitical activities.

Analyze the Data

Don't just rely upon headlines; delve into the information of marketplace reviews and information. Understanding the underlying facts can offer deeper insights and help you make extra knowledgeable selections.

Maintain a Long-Term Perspective

While market news and reports are crucial for quick-term buying and selling, it is also crucial to hold a protracted-term angle. Economic signs and company income reports can assist pick out lengthy-term tendencies and investment opportunities.

Manage Information Overload

The sheer quantity of marketplace news and reports can be overwhelming. Focus at the maximum applicable records on your buying and selling strategy and keep away from getting slowed down by way of much less crucial records.

Use Technology

Leverage era to streamline your analysis. Tools like financial information aggregators, sentiment analysis software, and economic indicator trackers can help you correctly process and interpret marketplace news and reports.

Economic Indicators and Their Impact

Economic indicators are information that degree diverse elements of a rustic's economy and are used to assess the modern-day and destiny health of the economic system. Economic signs can have a widespread effect on the stock marketplace, as the performance of the economy is carefully tied to the overall performance of the stock market. Investors and analysts pay near attention to economic indicators and use them to make greater informed choices about the stock marketplace.

Gross Domestic Product (GDP):

Gross Domestic Product (GDP) is a degree of a country's monetary pastime and is considered to be one of the maximum important indicators of a country's usual monetary health. The GDP is a degree of the cost of all items and offerings produced in a rustic in a given period of time, typically a yr or 1 / 4. When GDP grows, it commonly shows that the economic system is increasing and that agencies are developing, that can lead to higher corporate earnings and a stronger stock market. On the alternative hand, when GDP shrinks, it indicates that the economy is contracting and that businesses are suffering, which could result in lower company earnings and a weaker inventory marketplace.

If the GDP boom charge is better than expected, it is able to increase the inventory marketplace, while a decrease-than-predicted GDP increase price can cause a decline inside the marketplace. A robust GDP increase fee can indicate that the economy is on a strong footing and that the stock market is likely to hold to perform well, at the same time as a weak GDP growth price can imply that the financial system is slowing down and that the stock marketplace can be liable to a downturn.

Employment and unemployment fees:

Employment and unemployment fees will have a great effect at the inventory marketplace. High employment fees, or a low unemployment price, are usually visible as superb signs for the stock marketplace. When employment is excessive, customer spending is possibly to be strong, that may lead to higher company income and a more potent stock marketplace. Additionally, while unemployment is low, it suggests that there's a high call for labor, which could lead to better wages, which can also raise consumer spending, and in flip, raise corporate earnings and the stock market.

On the alternative hand, excessive unemployment quotes, or a low employment fee, can cause a decline within the inventory marketplace. When unemployment is high, patron spending is probably to be weak, that could cause lower company profits and a weaker inventory market. Additionally, whilst employment is low, it suggests that there may be a low demand for labor, that can lead to lower wages, which can also hose down client spending and in flip, decrease corporate income and the inventory marketplace. Investors additionally take note of the underlying traits in employment and unemployment figures, along with the rate of job introduction or destruction, in addition to the sectors which might be creating or losing jobs.

Inflation and Interest Rates:

Inflation refers to the price at which the fees of goods and services increase through the years, even as hobby quotes confer with the value of borrowing money. High inflation fees can cause a decline inside the stock marketplace. When inflation is excessive, it is able to indicate that the financial system is overheating and that there may be an excessive amount of demand for goods and services, which can lead to higher prices and a decline in consumer spending.

High inflation also can cause better hobby charges; as relevant banks will regularly raise hobby charges to try to reduce inflation. Higher interest costs can make borrowing extra pricey for businesses and customers, that can cause decrease funding and spending, which can in turn cause decrease company income and a weaker inventory marketplace. On the other hand, low inflation fees, and coffee-interest fees can enhance the inventory market. When inflation is low, it is able to indicate that the economy is strong and that there may be a healthful balance among deliver and call for. Low inflation can also result in lower interest fees, that could make borrowing cheaper for groups and customers. Lower interest fees can cause better investment and spending, that may in turn lead to better corporate income and a more potent stock marketplace. The coverage decisions of critical banks can offer perception into the health of the economic system and can help investors make greater knowledgeable decisions about the inventory marketplace.

International Trade

The stability of alternate refers to the difference between a country's exports and imports. A superb exchange balance, or sturdy exports, can raise the inventory market. When a country has a positive change stability, it indicates that there is strong demand for the united states' goods and services, that can cause better company earnings and a stronger inventory market. Additionally, a sturdy export market can indicate that the united states' economic system is healthy and that the country is aggressive within the global market. A negative exchange balance, or vulnerable exports, can lead to a decline within the inventory market. When a rustic has a terrible alternate balance, it indicates that there's vulnerable call for the use's goods and offerings, which could result in lower corporate earnings and a weaker inventory market. Additionally, a vulnerable export marketplace can suggest that the use's economic system is struggling and that the united states is less aggressive within the international marketplace. Investors also be aware of the developments in worldwide trade figures, including the path wherein the trade balance is headed, in addition to the exchange members of the family and agreements between nations.

Retail income

Retail sales seek advice from the whole sum of money spent on items and offerings by way of consumers at retail shops, each on line and offline. Strong retail sales are usually visible as a fantastic indicator of the stock market. When retail income is strong, it shows that purchasers are spending money and that the economy is healthful, that can result in higher company earnings and a stronger stock market. Additionally, robust retail sales can suggest that customer confidence is excessive, which also can improve the market. Susceptible retail income can cause a decline in the inventory market. When retail sales are weak, it suggests that purchasers are not spending money and that the economic system is struggling, that could lead to decrease company income and a weaker inventory market. Additionally, susceptible retail sales can indicate that customer confidence is low, which also can dampen the marketplace. Investors also be aware of the underlying trends in retail income figures, consisting of the route wherein they may be headed, as well as the sectors which might be riding or lagging in retail income.

Housing marketplace

The housing market refers back to the shopping for and promoting of houses and can include new creation, existing homes, and condominium houses. A robust housing market is normally seen as a positive indicator of the stock marketplace. When the housing marketplace is powerful, it shows that there's a high demand for housing and that the economy is wholesome, that could result in higher company profits and a more potent inventory marketplace. Additionally, a robust housing market can indicate that client self-belief is high, which can also enhance the market. When human beings are assured in their capacity to buy a home, they're more likely to shop for stocks as properly. On the opposite hand, a susceptible housing marketplace can lead to a decline in the inventory market. When the housing market is weak, it suggests that there is a low demand for housing and that the economy is struggling, which can cause decrease corporate income and a weaker stock marketplace. Additionally, a vulnerable housing market can indicate that purchaser self-assurance is low, which also can dampen the marketplace.

Integrating Fundamental Analysis into Your Strategy

To reach crypto or the Forex market buying and selling, you need a properly-rounded trading strategy. A strong approach combines numerous factors, along with technical analysis, essential evaluation, psychology, area, and emotional control. This offers investors a more comprehensive information of marketplace dynamics so that you can technique trades mindfully.

In this guide, we'll cover fundamental evaluation and why it's a cornerstone of trading. We'll also look at how you can contain the practice into your trading method.

What Is Fundamental Analysis in Trading?

Fundamental analysis approach comparing the underlying cost of a foreign money. To do a complete analysis, you'll want to bear in mind numerous elements that have an effect on a foreign money's fee, including:

The country's monetary regulations

Budget bulletins

Interest prices and inflation

Employment data

Political weather, elections, and pass-border tensions
Adverse climate events These elements act as catalysts for a unexpected bounce or dip in demand. A financial declaration mainly determines if the currency will witness a reversal or a breakout at the charts.

In crypto buying and selling, fundamental evaluation way going through the whitepaper to understand use instances and the adoption capability of a token. For example, buyers appearance closely at the block chain era, the undertaking's improvement team, partnerships, and regulatory surroundings.

Sentiment evaluation additionally plays a vital function here. Decisions through influential players, inclusive of banks and hedge funds, can notably effect crypto fees.

Qualitative and Quantitative Fundamental Analysis

There are two simple forms of essential analysis: qualitative and quantitative.

A qualitative evaluation seems at factors that may't be measured or counted to see how they impact the currency's cost. Examples consist of important news events, enterprise reports, social and political occasions, and marketplace sentiment. This will help you recognize the forex's long-time period potential. In quick, more political and monetary stability equals a more potent foreign money.

By evaluation, quantitative analysis is based on measurable and numerical facts, which include the u . S .'s gross domestic product (GDP), inflation charges (patron fee index), employment information, and alternate balances.

Overall, essential evaluation allows you recognize a currency's intrinsic fee compared to its modern-day market fee. If the intrinsic cost is better, then the asset can be undervalued. This affords a capacity buying possibility. But if the intrinsic price is decrease, it may endorse an overvalued asset, signaling a probable selling possibility.

How to Use Fundamental Analysis Effectively

Whether you're trading crypto or the Forex market, here's how you may gain a aggressive side with fundamental evaluation:

Crypto

Go through the whitepaper of a new assignment to evaluate the claims. This report will describe the mission's dreams, use cases, era, team, and future plans. Then, confirm the claims made within the whitepaper, as some initiatives may exaggerate or misrepresent statistics.

Look on the team behind the mission and notice in the event that they've worked on reliable projects before.

Are there similar projects in the equal space? Go thru the competition's whitepaper to look if the brand new token offers particular functions.

Look at its token omics. This will assist you recognize the token's software and distribution and notice whether the token has a clear call for.

What's the market capitalization, trading extent, and liquidity of this token? Market cap displays the asset's value, and liquidity guarantees that you may purchase and sell it simply.

The Forex market

Look on the macroeconomic elements for the us of a whose foreign money you chose. Is the economy booming? You can apprehend this by reading their global reserves and global debts.

Is the use of a politically solid? Does it have strong worldwide members of the family? A unstable political environment can result in huge forex fluctuations.

Create an eye fixed listing of currencies you want to exchange and observe their information and monetary calendars. This will come up with a schedule of upcoming monetary releases and occasions, along with employment reports or interest charge selections.

Combine the method with technical analysis to verify your findings.

Analysis To Earn Like TFT's Top Traders

Fundamental evaluation may be a complex exercise and can even seem educational. But when you grasp its primary ideas, it is able to emerge as a treasured tool to your buying and selling method. Economic records can inform you loads about how the forex will evolve within the long time.

A lot of traders on The Funded Trader use essential analysis to generate profits. Your goal as a brand new trader should be to first recognize the fundamentals of what drives the market. This will help you end up greater a success.

Chapter 6: Trading Psychology

Trading psychology describes how a dealer handles generating gains and coping with losses. It represents their potential to address risks and no longer deviate from their buying and selling plan. The emotional aspects of making an investment will attempt to dictate each transaction, and your capacity to handle your feelings is a part of your buying and selling psychology.

It is impossible to put off feelings in trading, however this need to no longer be the goal within the first region. Instead, investors must understand how certain biases or feelings can affect their buying and selling and use this fact to their advantage. Every trader is different, and there's no easy rulebook that everybody must comply with.

The fundamentals of dealer psychology

Fear and greed are effective feelings which can dominate the trader's thought method for the duration of their trading profession. The purpose is to learn how to harness these feelings and broaden a winning mindset.

A dealer can use numerous strategies to create a sturdy buying and selling psychology and maintain discipline. Besides analyzing books by using buying and selling psychologists and expert investors, you can additionally create a trading plan. Developing a trading plan will help you stick to a strong habitual and avoid attention gaps and loss aversion.

When starting to trade, feelings can honestly run amok. If an asset's rate actions speedy, a trader might begin to worry that they're lacking out. This is particularly so for newbie investors and is a regular emotion so one can often seem. Other emotions to manage are greed, worry of losing money, and the mental fortitude to triumph over mistakes which have been made. Last but now not least, one of the extra crucial components of developing a trading psyche is gaining knowledge of a way to manage risks.

Traders every now and then need to make snap choices. Even if you observe your buying and selling plan, there could be positive situations wherein you are compelled to make a brief decision. However, having a proper buying and selling approach and plan in vicinity will help you manipulate your feelings and make sure which you don't become making too many snap selections driven with the aid of your emotions.

Greed is some other most important hurdle many traders need to triumph over. The objective of trading is to generate income - or in different phrases, to make money. However, you need to have the right mind-set. Set a aim for yourself (for example, percent go back consistent with month) and work toward it. Never allow greed manipulate your actions.

A right manner to work to your buying and selling psychology is to in no way stop gaining knowledge of. Markets evolve all the time, and you could need to adjust your approach every now and then. You might also find which you in my opinion have modified as a dealer, which is why retaining a buying and selling magazine is invaluable.

The worry of lacking out (a.K.A. FOMO) is the feeling of missing out on a big possibility. If you hear from your fellow traders how much they have got earned by going long on Bitcoin, you is probably tempted to just blindly leap on the educate due to the fact you don't want to keep lacking out. This isn't the proper technique.

There will usually be opportunities inside the market, and you should input trades based totally in your buying and selling plan, no longer genuinely because you are frightened of missing out on a potential earnings.

The significance of growing a buying and selling psychology

One of the most important hurdles for each dealer is the worry of loss and making errors. Unfortunately, whilst trading, it is inevitable for one to take risks that could bring about losses. The emotion of fear of dropping out is otherwise called loss aversion. To triumph over this, a dealer wishes to approach their trading sports similarly to how a business is administered.

A correct method is to attention on information and referencing facts at the same time as preventing feelings from driving any buying and selling selections. Beginner traders must specifically don't forget constructing this dependency as part of their trading psyche before their first transactions.

Another method to develop a wholesome trading mindset is thru the creation of a routine. This ordinary can consist of a premeditated way of beginning the day. For instance, a trader would possibly recollect first of all catching up on information that turned into released while asleep. This could be observed by using checking your positions and reevaluating your chance control.

Improving trading performance is primarily based extra on the way you examine rather than what you analyze. Therefore, this reinforces the want for a recurring as it is key to mastering and understanding the proper way to alternate.

Trading mistakes and how they will negatively impact a dealer's psychology

One of the most commonplace buying and selling mistakes made by beginner investors is entering positions based totally on intestine feel, or intuition, while not having a particular approach. This arises from a lack of proper information and facts, which leads to a fear of probably lacking out on a golden opportunity. This ultimately results in the fear of dropping money and maintaining positions, which lets in losses to accumulate.

Thus, to keep away from falling into this vicious cycle, except having a buying and selling plan, a trader has to continue to be disciplined. Ensure that every trade undertaken adheres to the regulations or desires which have been outlined. Trading based totally on gut experience without a sound threat buying and selling plan is a mistake.

To keep away from those mistakes, you need to develop a danger management gadget, which determines:

Stop-loss stage

When to take income

Any capability trailing prevent loss

Indicators that help verify prevent loss levels and take earnings ranges

Getting right into a a hit buying and selling mind-set

Being able to undertake a a hit buying and selling mindset isn't always something that can be executed from the get-go. To expand a strong buying and selling mindset, it takes time and a sure stage of staying power to learn from successes and mistakes.

An excellent technique to useful resource this is to practice buying and selling with a demo buying and selling account. It will help in honing a very good trading psyche at the same time as allowing a trader to shine their trading skills and techniques. Most importantly, it comes without a chance!

By spending a positive amount of time trading on a demo account, will help a brand new dealer gauge the united states of America and downs of rate action, and the rollercoaster of emotions that includes whilst buying and selling, which ultimately allows to build self-belief.

As with maximum a success trader, do not let the concern of lacking out be the pressure to distract you from a trading approach. Staying disciplined is a essential psychological practice with a purpose to assist buyers gain achievement.

Can bias affect a dealer's psychology?

Yes, it can. Below we can take a look at some of the most commonplace biases that have an effect on buyers.

Gambler's fallacy People can misunderstand the idea of randomness. A correct example is roulette. The odds of the roulette ball falling on the coloration black are not growing just as it dropped on the pink shade numerous instances earlier than. The equal principle applies in buying and selling - just due to the fact you had five losing trades in a row doesn't mean that you are much more likely to hit a triumphing trade on the 6th attempt.

Anchoring bias An example of anchoring bias is if a trader is absolutely targeted at the charge of where they entered a exchange. This fee is completely beside the point to the rest of the marketplace, however it isn't always to the dealer.

Let's assume a dealer buys EUR/USD at 1.1950. The currency pair drops quickly after that, and the dealer keeps wondering "I just need the fee to go back to at least one.1950 and I can exit at breakeven". While 1.1950 becomes an crucial rate stage for our trader and he bases everything round it, the marketplace does its personal issue.

Hindsight bias If you have a look at a chart and try to visually pick out right exchange possibilities within the beyond, you'll locate plenty. The current pinnacle in the EUR/USD became "so apparent" - or the USD/JPY bouncing backtrack a certain aid level "couldn't were any clearer". We faux that things that already took place had been smooth to spot, however they had been no longer at that time. Especially if you perform under stress and actually need to click on on that purchase or sell button.

Confirmation bias Traders want to stay objective. When you're dealing with a dropping alternate, you should face truth and no longer simply are seeking proof that you are right and the market is moving inside the wrong path. This should turn out to be being an luxurious mistake.

Negativity bias Traders laid low with this have a tendency to assume a terrible final results in preference to a superb final results. While it isn't always terrible to stay cautious in trading, too much negativity can drain you and prevent you from pulling the trigger - even when there are great buying and selling possibilities to be had.

How to keep away from emotional buying and selling
It isn't always about getting rid of your feelings, but as an alternative about information and controlling them. To acquire this, a dealer should:

1. Have a stable trading plan You need to have a in reality defined plan - which machine you'll use (whether it's miles essential analysis, technical analysis, or a mixture of both), its advantages and downsides, how you'll identify trades, and the way you'll control them.

This desires to be accompanied by using a buying and selling magazine, where you can write down your observations, discover your weaknesses, and build on your strengths which assist you to avoid common trading mistakes and grow to be a profitable dealer. Jumping from strategy to approach will do no excellent and emotional buying and selling will take over.

2. Understand their hazard appetite Some traders is probably snug taking larger risks and control to preserve a groovy head even supposing they are going through a no longer-so-small drawdown. However, in case you are simply beginning or commonly have a decrease risk urge for food, that is not likely to quit well. You first need to pick out your very own threat appetite and plan hence.

three. Know while to take a wreck If you sense careworn and exhausted, you're much more likely to make errors or have interaction in revenge buying and selling. It can be a very good concept to set a rule for yourself as a way to define after what number of consecutive losing trades you will take a ruin and stop buying and selling until you have reviewed what took place.

After all, it isn't simply buying and selling which can purpose stress and cause a losing streak. There will be outside elements which can be having a bad effect on your mental kingdom, and it's miles possibly higher to take a smash from trading ought to you be dealing with this kind of scenario.

How to enhance your trading psychology?

Being able to expand and hone one's buying and selling psyche is closely aligned with achievement because it enables a trader to preserve calm in demanding marketplace environments. By acquiring a deeper expertise of the fallacies that would arise, sounder judgment will succeed.

However, to do so is not clean as buyers could make inferences which are noticeably subjective. It is always greater useful to examine data and utilize a device like PsyQuation. PsyQuation can assist degree a trader's overall performance and assist with this system to optimize future trading possibilities and assist traders make better decisions.

Other than that, it's also advocated for newbie traders to test out our buying and selling training as there are a plethora of articles that help new traders apprehend how trading works and increase a sturdy trading mindset.

Learning from Losses and Wins

In trading, each losses and wins provide treasured training which can substantially enhance a dealer's capabilities and overall performance. Understanding how to analyze and research from those experiences is crucial for non-stop development and long-time period achievement. This guide will explore the significance of learning from both losses and wins and provide sensible techniques for effectively analyzing and making use of these classes to your trading.

The Importance of Learning from Losses and Wins

1. Continuous Improvement
Each trade, whether or not a win or a loss, gives insights into your buying and selling strategy, selection-making system, and marketplace behavior. By studying those trades, you may discover strengths and weaknesses for your technique and make vital modifications.

2. Emotional Regulation
Understanding the emotional impact of wins and losses helps in developing higher emotional manage and resilience. Recognizing how emotions have an impact on your buying and selling choices can cause extra disciplined and rational trading.

3. Risk Management

Evaluating past trades enhances your hazard control abilities. By know-how the factors that caused losses, you could refine your risk control techniques to minimize future risks.

4. Strategy Optimization

Analyzing successful and unsuccessful trades allows you to optimize your buying and selling techniques. Identifying styles and factors that contribute to wins and losses can help you refine your techniques for higher performance.

Strategies for Learning from Losses

1. Analyze Each Loss

Take the time to thoroughly assessment every dropping trade. Ask yourself the subsequent questions:

What Went Wrong? Identify the specific reasons for the loss. Was it because of market conditions, poor execution, or a flaw on your approach?

Were There Warning Signs? Look for any alerts or indicators that could have predicted the loss. This should consist of technical indicators, information events, or market traits.

Was the Loss Preventable? Determine if there have been any steps you may have taken to keep away from the loss. This might involve better research, extra disciplined execution, or stricter adherence on your buying and selling plan.

2. Keep a Trading Journal

Maintaining a detailed trading journal enables tune and examine your trades. Record the following statistics for each trade:

Entry and Exit Points: Document the exact access and exit points, at the side of the motive at the back of those selections.

Market Conditions: Note the marketplace situations on the time of the change, including applicable economic indicators, information events, and technical analysis.

Emotions and Thoughts: Reflect to your emotions and mind earlier than, during, and after the trade. This can help perceive emotional patterns that impact your selections.

Outcome and Analysis: Summarize the outcome of the change and analyze the factors that contributed to the loss.

Learn from Mistakes

Mistakes are inevitable in trading, but they provide treasured mastering opportunities. Common errors to learn from include:

Overtrading: Trading too often or without a clear strategy.

Poor Risk Management

Failing to set forestall-loss orders or risking too much capital on a unmarried alternate. Chasing Losses: Trying to recover losses by using making impulsive trades.
Ignoring Market Signals: Overlooking vital technical or essential indicators.

4. Develop a Plan for Improvement

Based on your analysis, create a plan to cope with the problems that led to losses. This plan might encompass:

Refining Your Strategy: Adjust your buying and selling approach to cope with identified weaknesses.

Enhancing Risk Management: Implement stricter danger management guidelines, such as putting tighter prevent-loss stages or lowering function sizes.

Improving Discipline: Develop practices to decorate field, which include sticking to your buying and selling plan and keeping off impulsive selections.

Strategies for Learning from Wins

1. Analyze Each Win

Just as with losses, it's vital to investigate prevailing trades. Consider the following questions:

What Went Right? Identify the elements that contributed to the fulfillment of the trade. Was it due to market situations, accurate analysis, or effective execution?

Were There Risks? Determine if there were any risks or warning signs and symptoms that might have became the alternate right into a loss. Understanding these dangers helps in refining your strategy.

Could It Be Replicated? Assess whether or not the success of the trade may be replicated in future trades. Look for patterns or techniques that can be constantly implemented.

2. Document Successful Trades

Keep specified facts of your successful trades, inclusive of:

Entry and Exit Points: Note the exact access and exit points and the reasons behind those choices.

Market Conditions: Record the marketplace conditions on the time of the alternate, which includes relevant indicators and activities.

Emotions and Thoughts: Reflect for your feelings and thoughts for the duration of the trade to become aware of any high-quality emotional styles that contributed to the fulfillment.

Outcome and Analysis: Summarize the final results and examine the elements that brought about the win.

Identify Strengths

Successful trades monitor your strengths as a dealer. These might consist of:

Accurate Market Analysis: Ability to as it should be interpreting marketplace indicators and tendencies.

Effective Risk Management: Implementing effective chance management strategies that defend capital.

Emotional Control: Maintaining area and emotional manipulate during trades.

Reinforce Positive Behavior

Reinforce the behaviors and strategies that led to a success trades. This would possibly involve:

Developing a Checklist: Create a checklist of the important thing factors that contributed to a success trades and use it as a manual for destiny trades.

Building Confidence: Use a hit trades to build confidence in your buying and selling abilities and strategies.

Staying Consistent: Strive for consistency by using making use of the identical ideas and techniques that brought about beyond successes.

Balancing Learning from Both Wins and Losses

1. Maintain Objectivity
It's critical to remain goal whilst studying each wins and losses. Avoid letting feelings cloud your judgment and awareness at the data and data.

2. Avoid Overconfidence
While it's crucial to analyze from wins, avoid becoming overconfident. Overconfidence can lead to complacency and riskier behavior. Stay grounded and continue to observe your trading plan.

3. Embrace a Growth Mindset
Adopt a growth mindset, in which both wins and losses are seen as possibilities for gaining knowledge of and development. Embrace the method of continuous learning and improvement.

4. Regularly Review and Adjust

Regularly overview your buying and selling performance and modify your strategies primarily based on the instructions learned. Continuous development is prime to lengthy-term fulfillment.

5. Seek Feedback

Consider seeking remarks from different buyers or mentors. External perspectives can offer treasured insights and assist discover blind spots for your evaluation.

Chapter 7: Real-time Trading Strategies

In the fast-paced world of financial markets, the capability to make short, informed decisions can mean the difference between substantial gains and substantial losses. Real-time buying and selling techniques are crucial gear for day investors in search of to navigate the complexities of the marketplace with precision and confidence. These techniques leverage superior technology, actual-time records, and complicated analytical techniques to become aware of trading opportunities as they arise.

The essence of real-time trading lies in its immediacy. Unlike conventional funding strategies that target long-time period tendencies and sluggish appreciation, real-time buying and selling capitalizes available on the market's short-time period fluctuations. These dynamic surroundings call for investors to be constantly alert, equipped to act on the present day facts and execute trades within seconds. The intention isn't always just to expect marketplace actions however to reply to them right away, maximizing earnings from even the smallest rate changes.

Scalping Strategies for Quick Profits

Before we dive into a few precise scalping strategies, allows quick elaborate on what we mean by "scalping" and the function it performs in trading.

Scalping in trading entails making numerous trades over the course of a single day with the aim of capturing small income from minor rate actions.

Traders who hire this method, referred to as scalpers, normally enter and go out trades inside mines, seeking to take advantage of brief-term fluctuations in asset costs. Scalping requires a excessive level of field and the capacity to make quick decisions, because the fulfillment of this method is predicated on amassing a massive wide variety of small profits that together can upload as much as great profits over the years.

It also includes the usage of brief-time period charts.

In the context of "funded buying and selling," where traders are given capital by way of a funding issuer or corporation to change in alternate for a share of the income, scalping takes on a vast role.

Funded buying and selling packages regularly search for skilled traders who can generate consistent returns while managing risk effectively. Scalping, as a strategy, fits into this framework by allowing traders to take advantage of quick-term market actions to accumulate profits with the furnished capital, beneath the agreement that dangers are stored inside predefined limits.

The role of scalping in funded buying and selling is essential for numerous reasons.

First, it allows buyers to illustrate their potential to generate brief, regular income with strict chance control, a key metric for funded trading packages while evaluating a trader's overall performance.

The excessive volume of trades concerned in scalping permits investors to showcase their skill in studying the market and making fast decisions, that are treasured tendencies for any buying and selling approach however are especially important when using someone else's capital.

Secondly, due to the fact funded buyers are normally running within an earnings-sharing arrangement, scalping can be an attractive approach for generating some regular earnings circulate. By capturing small earnings throughout many trades, scalpers can intention to satisfy or exceed the overall performance benchmarks set by way of their investment companies, as a consequence maximizing their proportion of the earnings.

Price movement scalping method

The scalping strategy tends to cognizance on rate action simplest, and ignores all other fundamental elements that can have an impact on an asset's charge. This is an instance of technical analysis, in which scalpers examine price charts with scalping signs and other fee projection tools so that it will collect statistics on both beyond rate data and make future predictions.

Scalping may be compared to numerous other techniques of trading, maximum highly day trading and swing trading, due to their similarities of brief and brief-time period investments. However, these do no longer completely comply with the same techniques in the global of buying and selling techniques, so in what methods are they unique?

Scalping vs day trading

As we can infer from the name, day traders have a tendency to spend multiple hours on every change that they invest throughout the day, which can also provide an explanation for why each methods of trading have a tendency to overlap. Many use technical charts and indicators to awareness totally on the rate patterns of a financial device, searching at preceding changes within the marketplace to help plan for destiny trades. Similar to scalping, day buyers keep away from maintaining their bets open overnight, eliminating any in a single day exposure risk.

Scalping vs swing trading

In a similar way, swing trading is a less intense trading approach than scalping. Trades can be held for a few days, weeks or months, which suggests a much slower pace than each scalping and day trading. Traders additionally recognition on acquiring a smaller range of trades but with a bigger profit target. A slower pace blended with patience, analytical competencies and a much less disturbing surroundings make swing trading more suitable for novices and retail investors, at the same time as scalping is more appropriate to advanced experts.

High-frequency scalping approach

Scalpers tend to favor a market's volatility. High-frequency scalpers can use automatic software program to enter and exit masses of trades inside a fraction of a second, with the intention of taking pictures rapid charge fluctuations. Read more about high-frequency buying and selling here.

The foreign exchange market is in which a trader can discover a substantial majority of scalping possibilities. This is because the foreign exchange market has the very best buying and selling quantity and liquidity of all markets. This causes most important foreign money pairs to include tighter spreads than maximum markets, permitting investors to go into and exit positions speedy.

For instance, the uncertainty of Brexit and the United Kingdom's future in the European Union, together with latest well-known elections, had a bounding effect on the British pound. Forex scalpers intention to use this volatility to their gain via intently tracking the cost of the GBP inside the moments earlier than and after a important selection is made, prepared to hope on charge fluctuations.

Scalping shares

Traders use a stock scalping method sparingly, as the proportion marketplace can be very unpredictable. Although some stocks show growth potential, they might not all result in a point of liquidity that scalpers need if you want to input and exit a exchange with speed. In this situation, swing buying and selling shares is more usually used, as this employs a longer-time period approach, even as additionally trying to profit from small rate moves.

Swing Trading in Day Trading Context

Are you intrigued by using the concept of using the waves of the marketplace with swing buying and selling? This approach allows you to seize larger price actions over numerous days to weeks, diving deep into the marketplace's ebb and go with the flow. You'll discover ways to spot developments, use technical and essential evaluation, and expand a disciplined trading plan to ride the rate waves with confidence.

Perhaps you're interested in the quick-paced global of day trading? Here, you will thrive within the rapid lane, making cut up-second decisions to snatch small rate moves inside a unmarried trading day. You'll discover a way to navigate intraday volatility, use technical evaluation tools, and domesticate a focused mind-set to excel on this fast-fireplace buying and selling environment.

Or perhaps you're interested in unlocking the electricity of the futures marketplace? This marketplace offers some liquid surroundings for buying and selling standardized contracts on commodities, monetary gadgets, and currencies. You'll find the blessings of hedging and hypothesis, discover ways to control dangers with leverage, and leverage the liquidity of the futures marketplace for your benefit.

No remember which trading technique resonates with you, this guide will equip you with valuable insights and tools to be triumphant. You'll gain a deeper expertise of the strategies, dangers, and rewards related to every approach. Get prepared to embark on a journey to be able to empower you to capitalize on fee moves and reap your trading targets.

Ride the Waves with Swing Trading
Swing trading is your possibility to journey the waves of the market. As a swing dealer, you are now not simply

skimming the surface; you're diving deep to seize the big fee movements that span several days to weeks.

Spotting Trends in Swing Trading

You've been tracking crude oil costs and be aware they have got been oscillating inside a properly-described variety for weeks. You pinpoint the guide and resistance tiers within this variety. As the rate strategies the assist degree, you capture the instant and buy, watching for an upward swing.

You patiently preserve your position for several days, and because the price reaches the resistance stage, you promote, securing your earnings. You've simply mastered the artwork of using the price wave.

But how do you spot these trends? You'll want to keep an eye on marketplace information, economic signs, and geopolitical events which could affect the fee of the asset you are trading. Understanding the wider market context will let you count on fee actions and make greater knowledgeable buying and selling selections.

Tools for the Swing Trader

In swing trading, you'll harness the energy of both technical and fundamental evaluation to identify styles, trends, and signs that sign wherein the charge is headed. Tools like shifting averages, trend lines, and Fibonacci retracements allow you to become aware of potential access and go out factors.

But it is no longer pretty much the equipment. It's approximately how you use them. You'll need to increase a trading plan that outlines your entry and go out criteria, risk control strategies, and earnings goals. This plan will function your roadmap, assisting you live disciplined and focused to your buying and selling desires.

Your task? To seize large price movements than people who trade within a unmarried day, and to with a bit of luck hold positions in a single day. By combining the right gear with a stable trading plan, you will be properly-ready to journey the waves of the market and acquire your trading objectives.

Swing Trading Risks and Rewards

Swing trading offers the potential for massive earnings, however it also comes with dangers. You'll be retaining positions for several days to weeks, because of this you may be uncovered to overnight threat. Market situations can exchange rapidly, and sudden news occasions can cause sharp charge swings.

To control these risks, you may need to set prevent-loss orders to limit ability losses and take-earnings orders to fasten to your profits. You'll additionally need to monitor your positions regularly and modify your buying and selling plan as market conditions trade.

The rewards of swing buying and selling may be widespread. By taking pictures larger charge moves, you may acquire better profits than day buyers who awareness on smaller intraday price fluctuations. However, it is crucial to have a clean trading plan, manage your risks, and stay disciplined to succeed in swing buying and selling.

Thrive inside the Fast Lane of Day Trading

Trading in and out, or day trading, is your chance to thrive within the fast lane of the market. You're there for the short wins, making break up-2nd choices to snatch small charge moves within a unmarried trading day.

Navigating Intraday Volatility

Let's say you see a inventory it's been darting around with high volatility all morning. You zero in on a quick-term aid stage and get ready to pounce. As the stock nears the assist level, you spring into movement and purchase, expecting a quick bounce.

You set a decent stop-loss to protect yourself and a take-earnings order to lock on your profits. You hold a near watch, and because the stock hits your profit target, you go out. You've simply navigated the intraday charge action with precision and agility.

But how do you handle the stress of intraday volatility? You'll want to live calm beneath pressure, make short choices, and persist with your buying and selling plan.

It's crucial to control your emotions and avoid impulsive moves that may lead to pricey errors.

Techniques for Day Trading Success

For people like you who're drawn to the fun of day trading, there is no retaining positions in a single day; you're inside and outside, sidestepping in a single day danger. You'll lean heavily on technical evaluation, the usage of intraday rate charts, volume, and short-time period signs just like the Relative Strength Index (RSI) and Moving Average Convergence Divergence (MACD) to influence your speedy trading decisions.

But it's no longer just about the strategies. It's about the mind-set. You'll want to cultivate a disciplined and targeted approach to buying and selling, setting sensible income goals and sticking to your danger control strategies. By combining the right techniques with the proper mindset, you'll be nicely-placed to thrive in the fast lane of day trading.

Day Trading Risks and Rewards

Day trading gives the ability for short profits, however it also comes with risks. You'll be making fast-hearth choices, and the quick-paced nature of day buying and selling can be disturbing. It's vital to have a clear buying and selling plan, set prevent-loss orders to restrict ability losses, and take-income orders to fasten on your profits.

The rewards of day trading can be large. By shooting small fee moves within an unmarried trading day, you can acquire short profits. However, it's crucial to manage your risks, stay disciplined, and keep on with your buying and selling plan to succeed in day trading.

Unlock the Power of the Futures Market
Step into the futures marketplace, in which you may buy and sell futures contracts. A futures settlement is a percent between two events to buy or promote an asset at a predetermined rate on a destiny date. Traded on organized exchanges, those contracts are your gear for each hedging and speculation.
Hedging Your Bets with Futures
Consider a farmer bracing for a big wheat harvest in 3 months. The farmer frets approximately wheat

expenses plummeting with the aid of harvest time. To guard in opposition to this hazard, the farmer sells a wheat futures agreement at the cutting-edge market price, locking in a assured sale fee.

But hedging isn't only for farmers. It's for anyone who desires to shield against charge fluctuations within the underlying asset. Whether you're a commercial enterprise owner, investor, or trader, hedging with futures allow you to manage threat and attain more financial balance.

Speculating for Profit in Futures

Now, photograph yourself as a speculator having a bet on a upward push in wheat fees over the next 3 months. You purchase a wheat

futures agreement, hoping to offload it later at a higher fee for a tidy earnings. Both the farmer and you, the savvy speculator, are leveraging the futures market for your benefit.

But speculation isn't pretty much making a brief buck. It's approximately expertise the market dynamics, analyzing the factors that power price moves, and making informed trading choices. By staying knowledgeable and preserving a pulse on marketplace tendencies, you may be higher prepared to take a position for income within the futures market.

Liquidity in the Futures Market

The futures market is your playground, supplying some liquid surroundings with a numerous range of contracts, from commodities like oil and gold to economic instruments and currencies. The excessive liquidity of the futures marketplace lets in for quick exchange execution and tight bid-ask spreads, making it an attractive arena for investors such as you seeking to capitalize on rate moves.

But liquidity isn't pretty much velocity. It's about flexibility. The capability to quickly input and go out positions gives you the freedom to evolve to changing marketplace situations and seize new buying and selling possibilities. By taking benefit of the liquidity in the futures marketplace, you'll be properly-located to navigate the market with agility and capitalize on price moves.

Futures Market Risks and Rewards

The futures market gives the potential for widespread profits, but it also comes with dangers. Futures contracts are leveraged, which means that you may manipulate a large position with a incredibly small quantity of capital. While this leverage can extend your income, it is able to additionally magnify your losses.

To manipulate these dangers, you may need to apply stop-loss orders, set sensible income objectives, and display your positions frequently. It's critical to have a clear buying and selling plan, control your risks, and live disciplined to be successful inside the futures marketplace.

The rewards of buying and selling inside the futures marketplace can be great. By capitalizing on fee movements in commodities, financial instruments, and currencies, you may attain big income. However, it's crucial to manage your dangers, live disciplined, and keep on with your buying and selling plan to prevail in the futures market.

Charting Your Trading Journey

As you've explored the world of swing trading, day buying and selling, and the futures market, you have likely discovered that each method gives specific possibilities and challenges. The key to success lies in understanding the nuances of each strategy, growing a disciplined buying and selling plan, and staying targeted on your dreams.

Whether you are riding the waves of the marketplace with swing trading, thriving inside the fast lane with day trading, or unlocking the energy of the futures market, the adventure is yours to chart. Remember, there is nobody-length-suits-all method to trading. It's approximately locating the approach that resonates with your threat tolerance, time horizon, and trading objectives.

Now, we might like to pay attention from you. Are you a swing trader, day trader, or futures marketplace enthusiast? Or perhaps you are nonetheless exploring which technique suits you nice? Leave a comment under and proportion your buying and selling adventure with us. Let's analyze from each other and keep growing as buyers.

Chapter 8: Automation and Algorithms

Algorithmic trading (additionally called computerized buying and selling, black-container trading, or algo-buying and selling) makes use of a pc application that follows a defined set of instructions (an set of rules) to vicinity a exchange. The alternate, in concept, can generate income at a pace and frequency that is impossible for a human dealer.

The defined units of commands are based totally on timing, fee, amount, or any mathematical model. Apart from earnings opportunities for the trader, algo-trading renders markets extra liquid and buying and selling extra systematic by means of ruling out the effect of human feelings on trading sports.

How Algorithmic Trading Works

Suppose a trader follows those simple exchange criteria:

Buy 50 stocks of a stock while its 50-day shifting common is going above the 200-day transferring common. (A shifting average is an average of beyond statistics points that smooths out day-to-day price fluctuations and thereby identifies traits.)

Sell shares of the inventory whilst its 50-day transferring average is going beneath the 200-day moving average.

Using those simple commands, a laptop program will routinely screen the inventory price (and the moving average indicators) and location the purchase and promote orders while the described conditions are met. The trader no longer needs to screen stay prices and graphs or positioned within the orders manually. The algorithmic trading machine does this automatically with the aid of effectively identifying the trading possibility.

Advantages and Disadvantages of Algorithmic Trading

Advantages

Algo-buying and selling provides the subsequent advantages:1

Best Execution: Trades are regularly completed on the nice feasible expenses.

Low Latency: Trade order placement is immediate and correct (there's a excessive danger of execution on the preferred stages). Trades are timed correctly and right away to keep away from extensive charge adjustments.

Reduced transaction charges.

Simultaneous automatic assessments on more than one marketplace situations.

No Human Error: Reduced hazard of manual mistakes or mistakes whilst putting trades. Also negates human investors; tendency to be swayed through emotional and mental elements.

Back testing: Algo-buying and selling can be back tested the usage of available ancient and real-time facts to see if it's far a viable buying and selling approach.

Disadvantages

There are also numerous drawbacks or negative aspects of algorithmic trading to bear in mind:

Latency: Algorithmic trading is based on rapid execution speeds and occasional latency, which is the put off within the execution of a change. If a alternate is not achieved quickly sufficient, it can result in neglected possibilities or losses.

Black Swan Events: Algorithmic buying and selling is based on historical data and mathematical models to predict future market movements. However, unforeseen marketplace disruptions, called black swan activities, can arise, which can bring about losses for algorithmic traders.

Dependence on Technology: Algorithmic trading is based on era, along with computer applications and excessive-pace net connections. If there are technical troubles or failures, it is able to disrupt the buying and selling manner and bring about losses.

Market Impact: Large algorithmic trades could have a huge effect on market fees, that can result in losses for buyers who are not capable of alter their trades in reaction to these modifications. Algo buying and selling has also been suspected of growing market volatility at instances, even leading to so-referred to as flash crashes.

Regulation: Algorithmic buying and selling is issue to numerous regulatory necessities and oversight, which can be complex and time-consuming to conform with.

High Capital Costs: The development and implementation of algorithmic trading structures may be expensive, and traders may additionally want to pay ongoing expenses for software and information feeds.

Limited Customization: Algorithmic buying and selling structures are based on pre-described guidelines and commands, which could restriction the ability of buyers to customize their trades to fulfill their precise needs or preferences.

Lack of Human Judgment: Algorithmic trading is predicated on mathematical fashions and historical statistics, this means that that it does now not consider the subjective and qualitative elements that may influence market actions. This loss of human judgment may be a downside for investors who decide upon a greater intuitive or instinctive technique to buying and selling.

Building and Testing Automated Strategies

Lack of planning and ignoring the strategy section has value tens of millions to unique companies like Motorola, and every so often, they had to allow human beings cross or shut down operations on a product or a vicinity. While it can now not be the first element to do not forget whilst discussing a project concept or a brand new tech integration, the street ahead could be bumpy if check automation method and making plans are ruined. It works as a blueprint for the subsequent levels, and lots of duties take references from it.

Test Automation Strategy

Up till this point, it is pretty clear what we suggest with the aid of test automation and how did it come into existence. However, check automation today has grown a lot that we can't simply say, "We are choosing check automation". It is like pronouncing, "I power". But am I clean about what I power? Why do I pressure that? And what sort of car is it? Such questions are familiar in take a look at automation as properly. If you do check automation, what are your plans, and what tool? Why that tool? What type of automation? And it goes on and on.

To answer all these questions, we want to cautiously assess the software and what suits satisfactory for us. This is named a test automation strategy i.e. A strategy to put in force check automation into the software.

A test automation method is what occurs before the real check automation starts off evolved. It's the entirety that you have to look ahead to when you get stuck in the course of automation and the whole thing that will help you flow ahead to the subsequent step. For instance, if the automation approach states that at least 80% of take a look at insurance is needed, that can be regarded ahead to as a benchmark even as creating the checks.

Objectives of Test Automation Strategy

If growing a approach to automate your exams calls for such correct and comprehensive planning, will it not be extra time—and aid-ingesting than guide testing? While it could appear so, that's not what automation trying out method is all approximately. It is greater than making plans and updating.

It includes reusing the take a look at scripts to save time in constructing assessments, noting down the test desires to put off confusion from every meeting, and assembling the proper toolset to lessen your transport-to-market time by means of 30%.

Having a test automation strategy in region cautiously examines the regions to be examined and, consequently, improves the test coverage whilst accounting for the risks and obstacles one can also stumble upon at some stage in testing.

It turns interest closer to deciding on future-proof trying out tools and approaches that accommodate scalability and changes inside the software if brought.

A properly-built approach gets rid of multiple returned-and-forth between people and groups, smoothening their conversation.

Most of the time, regression testing takes the most important chunk of space, which may be decreased and managed with a great method in region.

Having a check automation strategy additionally makes it easier for each person to read and recognize the take a look at effects, which enables identifying and resolving problems.

Test Automation Strategy Example

While developing checks would possibly take days or weeks for some corporations, Quad wave started out doing it within hours.

As a global software program solutions organization, Quad wave spent several human assets and hours manually growing and jogging 8000-900 assessments for one assignment. They could end up blocking their weekends to deploy the builds that came on Friday.

Not a very good use of time, especially weekends!

But after implementing an amazing check automation approach and turning toward Test sigma to place that approach into action, Quad wave saw a outstanding shift of their output:

Created and ran over six hundred check instances in less than an hour.

Achieved 5x quicker QA automation

Got most check insurance for web, cellular, and APIs.

Free weekends!

What Happens Without Test Automation Strategies in Place?

First, let us delve into the results of not having a test automation method.

1. Failure to demonstrate commercial enterprise fee: When groups determine to put in force a brand new test automation solution, they regularly forget to bear in mind the enterprise motives for doing so. While the technology may be fantastic and potentially useful to the commercial enterprise, failing to tie it to actual commercial enterprise fee can result in the venture being canceled or no longer approved because of a loss of validated ROI or potential ROI.

2. Absence of foresight: Without a plan of action, it is hard to have a clean imaginative and prescient. Automation tasks frequently require pivoting, which

include bringing in a brand new software to automate or switching the framework generation. Without a documented vision, postponing or scraping the undertaking whilst confronted with a challenge is straightforward. You can determine the bigger pivoting questions and act accordingly with a clear vision.

3. Choosing the incorrect technology: Without a properly-described check automation approach, there's a hazard of choosing a wrong take a look at automation technology for your venture, ensuing in what's called "generation performance loss." Your test automation technology need to align with the software you're building. Failing to report this and broaden a approach can lead to attempting to force generation into an answer wherein it isn't suitable.

4. Unready for the "testing squeeze" Software improvement teams face a commonplace difficulty: the "testing squeeze."(in which trying out is just squeezed inside the leftover time without well planning and scheduling trying out sports) Despite the guarantees of Agile development approaches, this hassle persists. As a end result, it's far essential to have a stable test

automation method in place to determine which exams to prioritize. Without a clear understanding of what checks are maximum essential and tied to enterprise fee, teams may also scramble to make selections and cut the entirety. This method is inefficient and can cause enormous troubles down the road. Therefore, it's far crucial to have a well-notion-out plan in location to make sure that checking out is carried out successfully and successfully.

In end, having a properly-described take a look at automation approach is crucial to the achievement of any assignment. It ensures you can demonstrate commercial enterprise cost, hold a clear vision, maximize era efficiency, and be prepared for demanding situations.

What's the Purpose of a Test Automation Strategy?
If you're still thinking about the genuine purpose of a take a look at automation method, allow us to clarify.

The number one goal is to provide perception into a product or machine's hazard, abilities, and capability whilst setting up a dependable and repeatable method.

Also, a check automation approach communicates your dreams and plans to stakeholders. It may even spark discussions around new proofs-of-idea or technologies to put in force within your organization.

Lastly, it serves as an auditing tool, allowing you to study your preliminary plans and examine them in opposition to the real outcomes.

Implementing a check automation approach ensures that your merchandise and systems are very well tested and meet the very best excellent standards.

Benefits of Test Automation Strategy

When we provoke take a look at automation by means of first creating a plan and strategy, we achieve the subsequent advantages:

Faster take a look at automation: The take a look at automation method gives a blueprint for take a look at automation and steps to take for shifting beforehand. It helps facilitate the system quicker and works as a guide to wrap matters speedy.

Best for documentation: A test automation strategy highlights the whole thing that the test automation will work on. Therefore, if we document this, anybody related to the undertaking can get acquainted with the trying out process without going into technical info.

Helps in analysis: The take a look at automation method is planned before the real check automation takes region, however it's far exactly how our check automation might seem like. So, right here we will examine the dangers without investing any time in work and reworks and ensure we choose the route of minimal dangers.

Helps in reconfiguration: To maintain on the preceding factor, if somehow, we get stuck in the test automation phase and figure out that the course we chose has now not proved to be the excellent for us, we need now not analyze all our decisions via calling the team. Instead, we simply go through the method we accompanied and reconfigure it here, as everything we do is summarized in this document.

Provides a standard for the future: The check automation strategy is simply no longer for the modern-day testing section but may be observed for all destiny testing levels. Hence, the check automation strategy becomes a well-known for the organization, the crew individuals, and the brand new participants that join in the future.

Brings down prices: A quicker feedback cycle and faster reconfiguration approach we are saving time and investing it into other efficient matters. Everything associated to test automation method, consequently, saves time in a single manner or another.

How to Build Test Automation Strategy?

Finally, while we've accrued sufficient records approximately the take a look at automation procedure and the test automation method, it's time to understand the way to continue in developing one in detail.

Step 1 – Separate automation tasks with a clear imaginative and prescient

The first factor to understand in growing a take a look at automation method is the situations wherein this approach could be implemented. For this, we want to define clear boundaries as to what tick list needs to be surpassed for a scenario or a challenge to select for automation. It will assist in the modern-day in addition to all future checking out levels.

For a simplistic approach right here, we are able to recollect an action related to a sort of automation testing. Since those types had been developed with the need of automating those respective eventualities, it now not simplest facilitates us pick responsibilities for automation but also to which area it must be decided on. The following bullet listing may additionally help:

Repetitive tasks – The first trace of choosing a challenge for check automation is while it's miles going to be repeated numerous times in the future. For example, if on a specific URL, you need to check whether or not the remark phase or percentage works or no longer in every release, it ought to be computerized.

Large statistics inputs – The situations that want big records inputs to verify their capability ought to never be surpassed over to the manual trying out group. Consider a situation where 1200 login credentials want to be tested and the manual checking out group unearths a sure input not working. They send it returned to the builders, and they go back it by correcting it. However, considering a new change is driven, all 1200 credentials want to be examined, including those that exceeded in advance.

This is clearly an blunders-susceptible scenario and need to be decided on for statistics-pushed testing.

Multiple platform guide – Application that desires to be run on a browser and mobile OS need to be tested on hundreds of gadgets. The device marketplace is enormously fragmented, and we cannot depart a unmarried target device. Moreover, the devices keep acting in the marketplace often, which makes this mission ever-growing. Hence, considering the fact that comparable matters want to be repeated on a couple of devices, go-browser check automation is the right solution for it.

Verify strong functions – Features which have been released to the user are considered solid and are intended to continually stay so with destiny releases. But in software program development, no person knows what exchange may want to have an effect on which a part of the software program. Therefore, we constantly test the solid functions while liberating a new version. This will become a repetitive assignment.

If variations are launched in a month, hundreds of features with masses of their own situations need to be tested. Therefore, we positioned those responsibilities inside the automation basket precisely in regression checking out.

Scenarios leading to database alteration – Today's software program paintings heavily on the API machine to make adjustments to the database. These APIs are the backbone of any software program and consequently require thorough trying out. Every API should be selected to be included in the API testing section.

Tasks that cannot be examined manually – A few of the scenarios can in no way be automatic and surely, must in no way be. For instance, usability trying out is one such state of affairs that does not have a described sample. It simply explores the application like a user with the purpose of finding the defect. Automating this will risk the software and can ship insects into the released model.

Tasks which might be complicated and require longer time investments – At the begin of this submit we highlighted the motives why test automation got here into lifestyles i.E. To move matters quicker and take over repetitive tasks. If something is taking longer time to test and is complicated to setup, glaringly, we're bearing high expenses for it. Such duties need to be computerized.

These scenarios are the maximum generalized ones on the way to match any software program kind. However, we do agree with that from time to time a completely unique software can also ask for a completely unique set of protocols to pick what is going into automation and what does not. Do examine the business requirements to ponder over this list, because it might be beneficial in the subsequent checking out levels.

Step 2 – Build the crew

The maximum essential work in defining a take a look at automation strategy is to build a crew in an effort to work on it. If the crew is inefficient, even an appropriate technique cannot save the software program. However, there's no fixed pattern on the subject of building a team and plenty of things depend upon step 1 discussed above.

As a strategist, have a look at the finalized eventualities in step 1. For instance, if records-pushed checking out is included, a person who has worked in records-driven checking out and is aware of all of the instances that need to be examined need to be selected here. The talents of the team need to constantly suit the type of obligations the team is going to perform. Else, both the testing might also fail, or you can spend an excessive amount of time and costs in education the team.

If you have a set of contributors, you could forget about this step.

Step 3 – Choose an automation device

Now that we've decided on the eventualities and the team, it is time to pick an automation device that lies in sync with the above steps. For instance, if API testing is covered, now not only the group member should have experience in it, however additionally the device have to support it. So while choosing a tool, we want to carefully check the scenarios in addition to the familiarity of the group with the gear. The group must have earlier revel in in the usage of the tool to shop time in training charges.

However, considering the good sized variety of scenarios and the probability that not all team participants might choose a unmarried device without problems, this step will be hard to decode. A few predefined steps in this regard help, however if we examine the deeper facet of this trouble, the query isn't always about the tool in step with se however how the tool is used specifically. For example, all of the team individuals need to recognize programming, scripting, and all of the libraries and elements that help the tool goal factors inside the software program. The query is about whether a tool supports the language known to all of the group contributors. The query is whether all the crew individuals realize all the plugins utilized in checking out. So many questions cannot have a unmarried solution. Therefore, we flip toward something called a codeless test automation approach.

Codeless check automation is executing automation test scripts without writing any code, subsequently the word "codeless". The idea in the back of this technique is to put off the hurdles that come whilst we choose a device for the subsequent automation. If a tool need not have scripts, we want not ask the group individuals whether they recognize any programming language or not. As a result, a codeless test automation device can be used by anyone, every time, and in any challenge for the reason that it helps the automation scenarios finalized in step 1.

If you're a person who is simply beginning their journey with codeless check automation, the excellent tool to start with is Test sigma. Having used it for my part for my very own initiatives, Test sigma's great function is that it makes use of the English language to write down check automation scripts. Since English is widely known internationally, even though the crew contributors are located at distinctive geographical places, they are able to coordinate and write test cases pretty without difficulty. It additionally allows different gamers involved in testing, which includes shareholders and commercial enterprise analysts, to understand the take a look at automation and whether or not every in their eventualities is examined or not. Test sigma is geared up with all forms of test automation, which includes statistics-driven testing, API trying out, pass-browser testing, and lots more. For human beings required to test local mobile programs via acting moves at the app, Test sigma provides a cell take a look at recorder that statistics moves and converts them into check scripts.

It additionally offers actual devices for checking out. If we retrospect on our situation before getting to know approximately codeless take a look at automation, we discover that despite the fact that the team does not recognize something approximately a particular device like Test sigma, it wouldn't take a couple of day to study it. Since programming is removed, all this is left is to apprehend the device and its running to start. This is presently the excellent approach, and if viable, we advise you strive it as soon as for free by signing up at the platform. Always bear in mind that the learning curve and the ability to clear up complicated problems effortlessly is what makes a device worth of the use of in take a look at automation.

Best Practices to Build a Test Automation Strategy

Any test automation strategy works best when the right set of strategies is implemented. Simply having a listing of assessments and automating them to get the pass/fail outcomes does not represent a check automation method.

These fine practices will honestly make your subsequent check automation project a massive fulfillment.

Define Clear Objectives

Before you increase a plan for building, strolling, and reporting the consequences of you take a look at automation system, make sure to sincerely define the goals you want to obtain. It may want to variety from lowering the instances of guide effort and improving take a look at insurance to decreasing the checking out time and hard work. Whatever your plans are, note them down and follow the rest of the method as per the objective.

Create an Actionable Plan

Automation testing consists of more than simply walking a script and checking the output. In reality, maximum testers think that engaging in end-to-stop testing most effective constitutes take a look at automation, but that isn't always so. Unit trying out, integration trying out, UI checking out, and different testing kinds are also a part of automation. Make positive you formulate a plan that consists of a checking out pyramid and considers these types of different trying out sorts that may be automatic.

Choose the Right Tools and Frameworks

One of the most vital satisfactory practices of check automation method is to pick out the proper set of tools and frameworks that fit your test automation strategy. This option also depends upon the revel in and abilities of your checking out team. If they're cushy with a code-primarily based device, then cross for Selenium, Testing, Cypress, and Protractor. On the contrary, if your crew is quite new and seeking out new-age gear with codeless trying out capabilities, Test sigma, Testim, Katalon, Ranorex Studio, and Perfecto are a number of the best choices.

Similarly, your desire of framework will depend upon the wishes of the venture. Data-pushed, keyword-pushed, POM, Behavior-driven, and many more frameworks are a part of the check automation process.

Choose one or greater if they may be wished for the assignment you are operating on.

Design Maintainable Scripts

As we recognize, the software undergoes non-stop updates, which modifications its UI, features, and backend. Running check scripts to check the brand new functionality and the prevailing ones in such instances frequently effects in failed results. Creating maintainable take a look at automation scripts with self-restoration capabilities gives an simpler and extra handy way to keep the software program updates coming without spending time manually solving the exams.

Testsigma comes with the feature of self-heal tests that do not require protection.

Give your take a look at automation a lift with Testsigma

Select the Test Environment and Test Data

You want to be clean approximately in which you'll run the assessments, which includes the staging and production environments. Do now not overlook the want to switch and shop take a look at statistics inside the take a look at environment; use it as you carry out the trying out system.

Prioritize Tests Based on Risk and Impact

With a couple of testing types (move-browser, regression, integration, UI, useful) jogging for one software program, you will want so one can arrange and prioritize them primarily based on the risks and impact they bring about. If your software deals with exclusive records, together with financial or scientific information, safety testing takes precedence. Similarly, for an software that majorly issues itself with media gadgets, UI and useful assessments is probably essential.

Leverage CI/CD Integrations

Also, if you are looking into DevOps and the usage of CI/CD equipment to trap and clear up insects early in SDLC, choose tools and frameworks that provide such integration options.

Use Effective Reporting and Monitoring

The most vital part of the test automation strategy after defining the dreams and choosing the tools is reporting the results.

Make positive the computer virus reporting is free of technical errors and smooth for every person, such as stakeholders and non-technical individuals, to study and recognize. It should consist of the test details, including the quantity of checks achieved, pass/fail repute, pending test cases, the sort of exams run, and the studying from it. Any debugging facts or blockers have to additionally be protected in the test record.

Review and Update

Here comes the review and update part, which appears to be the never-ending challenge of any testing mission. Be it the assessments, the software, or the reviews, you would want to preserve all of them updated with any converting requirements.

If you are completely revamping your UI, it wishes to be up to date within the check script and in the objective. If your team is onboarding a new device, the equal desires to be added to the test automation method planning.

Whatever it's miles, any change from the original information have to be pondered in the method planning sheet proper away.

Focus on Skill Development and Collaboration

Lastly, do no longer forget the need to recognition on enhancing crew collaboration and abilities whilst enhancing the check automation manner. Following all the best practices to a good way to help your crew end up extra organized, efficient, and in song with their professional increase.

Pros and Cons of Automated Trading

Automated trading, additionally called algorithmic buying and selling or algo buying and selling, includes using laptop packages to execute trades primarily based on pre-defined criteria. This method has won sizable recognition amongst traders due to its numerous benefits, but it additionally comes with its own set of challenges. Understanding both the professionals and cons is essential for every person thinking about implementing computerized buying and selling strategies.

Pros of Automated Trading

Speed and Efficiency
Rapid Execution: Automated systems can execute trades within milliseconds, capitalizing on market opportunities faster than any human trader should.
Operational Efficiency: Algorithms can manage large volumes of trades, making sure regular execution without the chance of human errors or fatigue.

Elimination of Emotional Bias
Consistency: Automated trading eliminates the influence of feelings, including worry and greed, main to more constant decision-making primarily based on predefined rules.

Discipline: Algorithms follow their set parameters without deviation, preserving field in volatile market situations.

Back testing Capabilities

Historical Data Analysis: Traders can check their strategies in opposition to ancient marketplace facts to evaluate their potential overall performance earlier than deploying them in stay markets.

Optimization: Back testing permits for the refinement and optimization of techniques, improving their effectiveness.

Diversification

Multi-Asset Trading: Automated systems can manage and execute trades across a couple of markets and asset training simultaneously, improving portfolio diversification.

Complex Strategies: They can enforce complicated trading techniques that is probably challenging to control manually.

Time-Saving

Automation: Traders can shop widespread time because the device monitors the markets and executes trades on their behalf, letting them recognition on approach development and other obligations.

Cons of Automated Trading

Technical Failures

System Crashes: Automated buying and selling systems are susceptible to technical issues consisting of software insects, connectivity problems, and server outages, that could cause neglected possibilities or unintended trades.

Over-Reliance on Technology: Dependence on computerized structures may be unstable if investors aren't organized to intrude manually while important.

Over-Optimization

Curve Fitting: Back testing can once in a while cause over-optimization, in which the strategy is just too carefully tailor-made to historic statistics, ensuing in terrible performance in live buying and selling situations.

False Confidence: An over-optimized system would possibly give a false feel of safety, leading traders to underestimate real-global market complexities.

Cost

Initial Setup: Developing and implementing an automated trading gadget may be costly, requiring enormous funding in technology, records feeds, and infrastructure.

Ongoing Maintenance:

Regular updates and preservation are important to make certain the system maintains to characteristic successfully and adapt to converting market conditions.

Lack of Flexibility

Rigidity: Automated structures strictly adhere to their pre-described regulations, which can be a drawback in rapidly changing or unexpected marketplace conditions where human judgment might be superior.

Difficulty in Adapting: Adapting an algorithm to new market conditions or integrating new information can be complicated and time-consuming.

Regulatory and Ethical Concerns

Compliance: Automated buying and selling need to follow regulatory requirements, that can vary notably across distinct markets and jurisdictions.

Market Impact: High-frequency trading (a form of automatic buying and selling) has been criticized for contributing to market volatility and elevating ethical questions about marketplace fairness.

Conclusion

The Attention Trader: Strategies for Success in Day Trading" serves as a complete guide to gaining knowledge of the artwork of day buying and selling via the power of focused attention and strategic planning.

From the outset, we explored the crucial function of an attention dealer and the importance of preserving unwavering consciousness amidst the marketplace's volatility. We laid the foundational standards of day buying and selling, highlighting the essential gear, technologies, and the top-quality trading surroundings important for achievement. Building on this foundation,

we delved into the creation of personalized trading plans, the identity of key marketplace signs, and the implementation of robust hazard control strategies, underscoring the significance of capital preservation. Enhancing cognizance and field emerged as critical themes, with mindfulness strategies, based exercises, and strategies to triumph over distractions forming the backbone of a disciplined trading technique. The eBook furnished an in-depth exploration of technical and fundamental analysis, equipping traders with the capabilities to interpret chart patterns, traits, economic reviews, and integrate those analyses right into a cohesive trading strategy. Trading psychology become addressed, emphasizing the management of emotions, development of a resilient mind-set, and the capability to learn from each losses and wins. Real-time trading techniques, along with scalping, momentum trading, and swing buying and selling, had been tested, offering numerous processes to capitalize on marketplace opportunities. The introduction to algorithmic trading and the construction and trying out of computerized strategies highlighted the intersection of generation and buying and selling, while the discussion on continuous development stressed the importance of ongoing training, change review, and staying up to date with market changes. Finally, case studies and actual-international examples furnished useful insights from a hit buyer, illustrating sensible applications of the strategies discussed and lessons from first-rate marketplace occasions. As you move ahead, recollect that success in day trading is a adventure of perpetual learning, disciplined execution, and adaptive techniques.

Stay centered, hold refining your capabilities, and permit the standards and strategies mentioned on this eBook manual you in the direction of reaching your buying and selling aspirations inside the dynamic global of day buying and selling.

www.ingramcontent.com/pod-product-compliance
Lightning Source LLC
Chambersburg PA
CBHW072050230526
45479CB00010B/473